An Eye For An Eye

Makes

The Whole World

Blind

Poets On 9/11

An Eye For An Eye Makes The Whole World Blind

Poets On 9/11

Edited by
Allen Cohen & Clive Matson

Foreword by
Michael Parenti

REGENT PRESS
OAKLAND, CALIFORNIA

11/12/03

Library of Congress Cataloging-in-Publication Data

An eye for an eye makes the whole world blind: poets on 9/11 / edited by
Allen Cohen & Clive Matson; foreword by Michael Parenti.
     p. cm.
     ISBN 1-58790-034-3
          1. September 11 Terrorist Attacks, 2001--Poetry. 2. American
poetry--21st century. 3. Terrorism--Poetry. I. Cohen, Allen. II. Matson,
Clive, 1941-

PS595.S47 E98 2002
811'.6080358--dc21

                                                      2002030688

Cover Image by Frank Bella • www.bellastudios.com
Image on back cover by Carolyn Ferris

Manufactured in the United States of America

REGENT PRESS
6020-A Adeline Street
Oakland, CA 94608
regentpress@mindspring.com

First Edition 2002

This book is dedicated to all those who have given their lives
in the wars that have held humanity hostage
to the recurring nightmare of history
and to those dreamers who can see and manifest
a new world of peace and justice for all beings.

One day the sun admitted
I am just a shadow.
I wish I could show you
the Infinite incandescence
that has cast my brilliant image!
I wish I could show you
when you are lonely or in darkness
the astonishing light
of your own Being!

—Hafiz – 14th century Persian Poet Rendered by Daniel Ladinsky

Each of us inevitable.
Each of us limitless - each of us with his or her right upon the earth;
Each of us allowed the eternal purports of the earth
Each of us here as divinely as any is here.

—Salut Au Monde - Walt Whitman 19th century American Bard

Table of Contents

Introduction

On Tuesday morning, September 11, 2001, the skyscraping World Trade Center in New York City and the Pentagon in Washington, DC were attacked by our own hijacked commercial airliners before the TV eyes of the entire world. America grieved for its losses but its innocence and idealism were also wounded.

Since then there has been an unrelenting bombardment of events beginning with the President's declaring war on the Islamic terrorists and Afghanistan, the anthrax scare, the rescinding of some of our constitutional rights, the revelation of FBI and CIA intelligence incompetence, the rising intensity of the Palestinian and Israeli conflict, the revelations of corporate corruption, the stock market's precipitous drop, a recession and increased unemployment and the proposed invasion of Iraq. Have I left anything out? Oh, yes! Global warming, drought, plague and fires throughout the Western U.S., and floods in Central Europe.

Yet the American public seems comatose or hypnotized by the combination of propaganda and spin coming through the corporate controlled media, presidency, and congress. Independent and dissenting views are rarely heard. It was in this atmosphere that I felt it necessary to gather the voices of America's poets to establish a different historical record of these monumental events. A record based on the perceptions and feelings that can be uniquely mirrored in the poem.

This Anthology began as an idea in an email correspondence in mid-May 2002 that resulted in a call for poems broadcast over the Internet. It is a manifestation of the enormous fluidity of communication that is possible through the Internet despite the limitations to the free flow of communications in the monopolistic mass media. It makes me think that we are only at the beginning of using the Internet for social change as long as we can maintain its freedom of use.

Occasionally I would send poems by email to Clive Matson and others as a form of immediate poetic communication. In May he sent me his poem on 9/11 *Towers Down* with a note saying that Diane di Prima was thinking of publishing her poem on 9/11 with his in a small chapbook. I answered that there were many fine poems on the subject around including poems by Lawrence Ferlinghetti and Jack Hirschman and maybe we need to do an Anthology.

Clive said he was really too busy. So I suggested that he put out the word through his personal and Internet connections and I'd receive and read the manuscripts. Little did I know that in a few weeks I would be deluged with almost a thousand poems. Thanks Clive! So many poems came in that my C drive crashed. Luckily the poems were backed up on another drive.

I was surprised upon reading the poems that ninety percent were good poems. They expressed deep emotions and profound thoughts with the severe attention to detail that makes poems revelatory, and each poem had its personal music and rhythm.

Usually when I edited the *San Francisco Oracle* or have judged poetry contests, I could discard the majority of poems after reading the first few lines. But the attack on the Towers and the horrific death of so many innocents and the implications for the future of America and the world had riveted the artistic imagination of many poets and they produced a consistently important body of work.

Many of the poets had projected themselves into the minds and the bodies of the victims of 9/11, and the firemen and policemen who were searching the wreckage of the buildings and even the suicided hijackers. It brought to mind the concept of Negative Capability originated by the 19th century romantic poet, John Keats in a famous letter to his brothers:

> *…when a man is capable of being in uncertainties, mysteries, doubts,*
> *without any irritable reaching after fact and reason—*

These poets had thrown their consciousness into lovers talking on the phone for the last time, a fireman wondering how he would say grace at Thanksgiving dinner after digging up limbs from Ground Zero, and especially the people who threw themselves from the high floors of the World Trade Center rather than be smothered or burned in the advancing smoke and fire. Their poems hover there in the mystery of death and chaos, grief and anger.

Other poems confronted the political, existential and metaphysical problems that had suddenly exploded in the American psyche with great sweeps of high rhetoric, metaphor and even rap rhythms.

Just after 9/11 I had co-edited a newspaper called *Peace News* with John Bryan, one of the veterans of the underground press movement. Paul Krassner, the editor of the Realist and renowned social satirist, sent us an article that began with the line, "From now on everything will be divided between what happened before the events of September 11, 2001 and what happened after." This idea at first didn't catch me as being either true or relevant despite its being echoed everywhere. I thought it would blur the important historical roots of the dilemma we now faced.

But upon reading these poems written by so many diverse poets, I see a deepening of perception, of renewed seriousness about the human predicament and about the necessity to evolve into our full humanity. If the poets are the canary of consciousness or as another 19th century romantic poet, Percy Bysshe Shelley said "the unacknowledged legislators of the world," this experience of vulnerability might be the harbinger of a new maturity for the American civilization.

To say this may seem overly optimistic in the face of the suppression of constitutional rights, the possibility of more suicide attacks, the corruption of corporations, rising unemployment, deficiencies in health care, the rule of the oligarchs and the din of propaganda inducing a collective uniformity, but the poets are singing and they are seeing a new world.

So I must thank the over 800 poets from the US, England and Australia who have sent their work to us for sharing their sorrow, grief, anger and hope. I hope the poems chosen for this book will help their readers to feel more deeply, and think about our future and ultimately act to achieve a more peaceful and just world.

— *Allen Cohen*

Preface

Since the tragedies of September 11, 2001, we haven't had a clear public voice for the body politic. I hear war talk, recalled horror, and patriotic clichés that all seem like armor covering an uncomfortable wound. "One wonders if nature — instinctual wisdom," Adrienne Rich wrote of a poet, "— might not have led him to drop the greaves and breastplates of those old warriors and to step, finally, light and self-exposing, into the fray." Even several voices, however different, speaking with that self-exposing honesty, would be a monumental relief.

This country has embraced a veneer of righteousness as its armor. From the day the administration called the terrorist attacks "acts of war," that righteousness has drummed through public consciousness. The president made his declarations, congress followed suit and upped the ante, international law was ignored, the military geared for action, and mainstream media dismissed any dissent.

What underlies this veneer? That's not easy to determine, since the righteousness accelerated quickly into a "din of collective madness," as Allen Cohen observes. Shock and anger have taken over and drowned out the heart. And how can we hope to think and act with integrity, if we don't know the voices within us? That's the first wish for this anthology: to become a forum for those voices.

I cherish Robert Hass's conviction that "poetry is at the very core of the culture." A year after September 11 grief is still central, but it's skewed. So little grief is expressed for foreign dead, and so much for our dead, that grief seems a justification for more bombing. The fact is, I think, that we've plunged into a chaos underneath the grief. A chaos of horror, of anger, of doubt, of poorly formulated guilt, of despair, of loss of the comfortable self, of feeling something's terribly wrong.

It's natural, of course, for people to have huge responses to the attacks. We are a passionate people — witness rock music, football, space heroes, flappers, all the way back to tea rotting in Boston Harbor. We honor gut responses. But it's not appropriate to act impulsively. We have no excuse; we are no longer a young country expanding into a continent where we proceed, seemingly, without consequence. We are part of a world community and everyone knows it: it's the 21st century. Anything we do has repercussions. In fact, September 11 is itself a repercussion — of an ugly situation created throughout the developing world.

The media say people support the U.S. government. But how do those who believe, "There must be a better way," answer the pollsters? How do you answer a question posed with the facts: "Do you support the war on terror as it is being carried out, even though Afghanistan is in shambles, hundreds of thousands more Afghans now living in tents; even though Osama bin Laden has not been apprehended; even though Al Qaeda has probably become more popular; even though twice as many innocent people have died by U.S. bombs than on September 11; even though the war has put our future and our children's future in hock?" The people of the U.S. are not dumb. We do not, certainly not to the extent the polls suggest, support the war on terror.

Slanted polls help that righteous armor permeate the culture, and the Vietnam War demonstrated very well how opinion gets manipulated. Is this knowledge being applied today? Aside from Pacifica Radio and a few journals, we don't have a forum with real discussion of issues. What can be done? What can we do, when the president talks about using nukes on a half dozen nations and sending the military into Iraq on his own?

In a positive sense, September 11 gives the U.S. a chance finally to come of age. The Friday after September 11, Gail Ford went ahead with her monthly poetry gathering. She noted the same thing Dana Gioia remarked in his essay, "All I Have is a Voice": his speaking tour and her salon were rather exceptionally well attended. People came to be in the presence of poets, who were expected to approach the event in a real fashion, even if this meant expressing doubt and confusion, perhaps because doubt and confusion would be expressed.

Clear understanding of political forces can help. But the most forceful cracks in the veneer, I believe, will be made by information in our hearts, thrusting upward. Some material from our wounds, some knowledge of being human, some understanding of pain and consequences, must be able to break through. Surely the armor, all that fear and shock and need for revenge, is vulnerable. I look for a bursting up in the individual and in the body politic. It would be most natural for poets to help with the words.

The call for poems for this anthology went to email lists, to all the poets Allen Cohen and I know, and to almost 200 of the better-known poets in *Poets & Writers*. Everyone was asked to forward the call. Even with this wide net, many fine poets were left out, partly because the time was so short, partly because some poets list with publishers — many of those letters came back "forwarding order expired" — and partly because the poetry world is segmented. Poets seem to form affinity groups that don't overlap easily: Language poets, Spoken Word poets, and academic poets are not fully represented. The poems here are drawn from half or perhaps two-thirds of the poetry world.

One poet even expressed doubt that linking poetry and September 11 is valid. To be sure, much 20th Century poetry has been a sanctuary for alienated and gifted sensibilities. By a similar token some poets admit inability to find words for such a terrible event. September 11 is, nevertheless, a call for poets to reclaim our oldest, most basic tradition: giving identity to — and thereby healing — the unknown and the chaotic. This role dates back to 2,000 BC in the Greeks, 7,000 BC in Sumeria, and probably for 35,000 years of human consciousness.

That tradition has generated at least one book already: William

Heyen chose prose writers and poets for *September 11, 2001: American Writers Respond* (Etruscan Press, Maryland, 2002). "O Books" is also preparing a journal "Enough", and the activist group "Poets For Peace" has a collection in progress. The present anthology is another step, hopefully a large one; *An Eye For An Eye Makes The Whole World Blind* is a gathering place.

The voices here do not show unity. They show passion, grief, outrage, dismay, hopelessness, all the difficult stuff. The contradictions and the dissent are not unpatriotic, they're real. And the power of the words demonstrates that, all along, the poets have been doing their jobs. But our culture has been ignoring the poets. How many people know, for instance, that at the onset of the Gulf War, Robert Bly led his workshop out into the streets of Los Angeles in a grief march?

If the U.S. government invades Iraq, that will be a rallying point for dissent — a very late one. We are a much smarter people if we act sooner. Who shall we be, in the next period? To take in these voices — to listen and honor any resonance — is to exploit the role of poets properly. Righteousness is almost everywhere. If the sentence I posed for the pollsters provokes disbelief, the veneer has permeated dangerously far. The poets' 35,000-year-old tradition is in the reader's body, too, under the veneer. Perhaps only a thin skin needs to be split away.

I have great hopes for this anthology. I believe words and images have the power to define the chaos we're floundering in. A multiplicity of poets is working, each in different ways, throughout these pages with just the required honesty. And the day that spawned their poems couldn't have greater impact on our lives — perhaps couldn't have greater impact on the future of the planet. The reader will discover how worthy these voices are of Adrienne Rich's insight, stepping "... light and self-exposing, into the fray."

— *Clive Matson*

Foreword

On the morning of September 11, 2001, terrorists hijacked four US commercial airliners and managed to plow two of them into the twin towers of New York's World Trade Center and another into the Pentagon. The fourth plane crashed into the Pennsylvania countryside. Some 3000 lives were lost that day. In the immediate aftermath of this tragedy, almost-elected president George W. Bush announced his "war on terrorism."

To most of us, September 11 was horrifying. To the people in the White House, it was a golden opportunity. Bush himself said as much, announcing that "this may give us an opportunity we didn't have before." Indeed, it was an opportunity for him to advance the agenda of the reactionary Right at home and abroad. This included rolling back an already mangled federal human services sector, raiding and eliminating the Social Security budget surplus, pushing through new tax cuts and reverting to deficit spending for the benefit of a wealthy creditor class, increasing the repression of dissent, and expanding to a still greater magnitude the budgets and global reach of the US military and other components of the national security state, while launching a one-sided war against yet another impoverished and defenseless nation.

September 11 had a terrible shock effect on the millions of Americans who get all their news from the corporate media and who were secure in the belief that everyone in the world secretly wants to be an American. Our citizens believed that our nation was universally loved and admired because it was more prosperous, nobler, and more generous than other countries. Very few Americans know about the victims of US state-sponsored terrorism throughout the world. Relatively few are aware that whole societies have been shattered by US bombings or US monetary and trade policies. They are shocked—and skeptical—to hear that US imposed economic sanctions keep people in misery in Cuba, Iraq, North Korea, and Yugoslavia. They have little sense of how free-market deregulation, privatization, and cutbacks on human services—imposed by the IMF, the WTO, NAFTA, GATT, and other "free trade" agreements—are diminishing the life chances of millions of people in countries around the world.

And not many of our citizens know that US power has destroyed democratic mass movements throughout the Middle East and in Central Asia, in countries like Turkey, Iraq, Iran, Egypt, Syria, and Afghanistan. Generally Americans believe that US interventions across the globe have been benevolently motivated, dedicated to peace, democracy, and human rights—just as their leaders have been telling them.

Then, along came these September terrorists who had gained entry into this country and could have applied for citizenship, but instead chose to commit mass murder and suicide, sending us the message that we and our country, and what it represents, are horribly despised. It was all extremely unsettling to many of our compatriots. What changed on September 11 was their perception of themselves and of America's place in the world. Many felt shocked, smaller, not respected, powerless, and confused. Some even wondered if there were things they had not been told.

The entire nation and indeed the entire world knew about September 11 because of the repeated play it was given in the US corporate-owned global media. In contrast, much of the world and almost all of America know next to nothing about how US-supported terrorists have taken millions of lives in scores of other countries. Very few people know about the role the US national security state has played in the death of over a million people in Angola and some 900,000 in Mozambique, or the hundreds of thousands killed in Indonesia and later on in East Timor, or the tens of thousands exterminated in Guatemala and El Salvador by death squads and military forces trained and financed by the CIA and the Pentagon. The media have little to say about *those* acts of state-sponsored terrorism, and so the general public knows relatively little about them.

The media and our public officials have even less to say about *why* such criminal interventions have been perpetrated, what interests are being served, at whose expense and for whose gain. Media pundits prattle on about building democracy abroad, defending "US interests" (left undefined), fighting terrorism, assuring "stability," and the like. They say little about how they strive to make the world safe for the Fortune 500 and for international financial investors, little about how they have systematically targeted popular reformist movements throughout the world, exterminating peasant leaders, trade union organizers, dissident clergy, student protestors, and even whole communities and regions because the people in those places tried to take a path different from the "developmental free market" model offered by the forces of corporate globalization.

In July 2002, the prestigious Council for Foreign Relations reported that many people throughout the world saw the United States as "arrogant, hypocritical, and self-absorbed." US global power was less admired than feared and hated. US policies abroad were experienced not as the offerings of a democratic republic but as the bitter fruits of a repressive empire. It would have been too much to expect the council, given its semi-official status, to call for a critical appraisal of US policy and for drastic changes in goals and interests. Instead, it treated the issue mainly as a public relations problem. The US would have to do "a better job of selling itself." No thought that there was something wrong with what was being sold.

When our leaders continue to serve the special interests of those who control the land, labor, capital, natural resources, and markets of this and almost all other nations, when they continue to violate the humanity of everyone else at home and abroad, then it is time to raise our voices against the subterfuge, the hidden agendas, and the heartless imperatives of empire. And then it is time to turn to the poets. The selections in this volume offer a rich trove of imagery, insight, and protest, not only about September 11 but about much that came before and has happened since. This fine collection of poems ranges over a broad spectrum of issues, both political as well as personal, often both at the same time. The task of the dissident political analyst is to relate immediate issues to larger sets of social relations and to the hidden history and deceptive politics that too often remain unspoken. As is demonstrated in the pages ahead, in a different way and with much heart, this is also what the better poets do.

— *Michael Parenti*
author of The Terrorism Trap: September 11 and Beyond

POETS ON 9/11

HISTORY OF THE AIRPLANE

And the Wright brothers said they thought they had invented
something that could make peace on earth (if the wrong brothers didn't
get hold of it) when their wonderful flying machine took off at Kitty Hawk
into the kingdom of birds but the parliament of birds was freaked out
by this man-made bird and fled to heaven

And then the famous Spirit of Saint Louis took off eastward and
flew across the Big Pond with Lindy at the controls in his leather
helmet and goggles hoping to sight the doves of peace but he did not
Even though he circled Versailles

And then the famous Flying Clipper took off in the opposite
direction and flew across the terrific Pacific but the pacific doves
were frighted by this strange amphibious bird and hid in the orient sky

And then the famous Flying Fortress took off bristling with guns
and testosterone to make the world safe for peace and capitalism
but the birds of peace were nowhere to be found before or after Hiroshima

And so then clever men built bigger and faster flying machines and
these great man-made birds with jet plumage flew higher than any
real birds and seemed about to fly into the sun and melt their wings
and like Icarus crash to earth

And the Wright brothers were long forgotten in the high-flying
bombers that now began to visit their blessings on various Third
Worlds all the while claiming they were searching for doves of
peace

And they kept flying and flying until they flew right into the 21st
century and then one fine day a Third World struck back and
stormed the great planes and flew them straight into the beating
heart of Skyscraper America where there were no aviaries and no
parliaments of doves and in a blinding flash America became a part
of the scorched earth of the world

And a wind of ashes blows across the land

And for one long moment in eternity
There is chaos and despair

And buried loves and voices
Cries and whispers
Fill the air
Everywhere

— *Lawrence Ferlinghetti*

NEWS FEEDS

1. last rites

my ears are full
the building screeches
smoke and heat
my skin blisters
i'm going to die
windows open
i'm going to fly

dust rises
nothing but smoke
gray turning black
turning white
i am blind
i can see an opening
window frame and clouds
i'm going to fly
i'm going to die

i'm going to fly
wind in front and air
that my lungs can clutch
i'm going to fly
screams in back
and a wall of fire

i'm going to fly
i love my life
i'm going to fly
i love the sky
i'm going to fly
my god my dear sweet god
i'll kiss your ground
i'm going to die

2. ray's howl

my niece she was so young
her eyes so bright shining
on a moonless night
kill them
kill them all
kill them
kill them all

she rode her bike
up and down those streets
not a job for a girl
i always said

she made me laugh
from the first day i saw her
soft hair toothless grin
smooth pink skin

so innocent my niece
so full of life
headstrong
to choose new york
over california

not a mean bone in her body
no hate in her soul
kill them kill them all
kill their families
decimate their memory
they have killed my niece
all of them

and you who would
point a finger of blame
at this nation
look at our stars
our flag waving broadly
the red is for blood

and you who would
talk of roosting chickens
and debts repaid
you who would say
we america brought this on
kill you too kill you
kill you all

no hate within her soul
no bitterness on her tongue
no blame she held no blame
kill them
kill them all
bomb their villages
wipe out their memory
let no one know they ever were

my niece so young
so sweet so kind
kill them kill you
kill them all
kill them kill you
kill you all

3. 911

911 911
nana is in san francisco weeping
she can not find her eldest girl
who runs down wall street
stepping over dead bodies
tears washing concrete soot
from her dark round eyes
her lover jumps in front of her
wards off the explosion of glass
pointed at her model's face
sleek smooth pecan brown
he is cut he is slashed

'he bleeds as they run
and weep
as nana cries out in fear
in relief in praises when
she hears her daughter alive
amidst so many deaths

911 911
jaci cannot find her sister
she is having dreams
that turn colors
and leave mirages of touching
but the phone hasn't rung
so she writes poems inside her fear
and we pray and we pray
louder and louder
but the phone stays silent

911 911
pamela puts her arms around a child she does not know
who sits in the office of a small new jersey school
my mother works in new york the child weeps
and i don't know where
pamela doesn't say it will be alright
she says we'll find out baby
we'll find out

911 911
it has only begun
a first salvo some say
scripture armageddon
vengeance is mine says the state
vengeance is ours say the newscasters
but the dead will still be dead
and the wounded forever scarred
and thousands of families
torn and crippled

and people keeping jumping

out of skyscraping windows
falling like stringless puppets
to the dust covered ground below

i keep watching them fall
as if somehow being witness
will make it better
and the planes cutting through
concrete glass and iron
and the fire and the smoke
projected again and again
in an endless loop
the buildings melting to powder
the people covered in white
like an african death ritual
powdered skin and hair and cloth
eyes open and unblinking

911 911
emergency
world emergency
here
and here
and here
we are all terrified
we are all terrorized
we are all reduced
to rubble
needing to build again
911
911
911

4. aftermath

checking in
i am safe
checking in
i am praying

checking in
i have faith
checking in
i am working
for a justice built
on food and equity
checking in
i am struggling
for a peace
built on land and family
checking in
checking in
i am seeking
a righteousness
built on humanity and sweat
and a future
built on love
and memory

— *devorah major*

AMERICA ON TERRORISM

1.
i was a child
when i first saw the pictures
black men's bodies
hanging from trees

castrated
burnt
picnic
laughed
the men and women
with their children

nigger cookout
some of them seemed to speak
into the camera lens
the smell of burnt flesh
fresh in their nostrils

i've been against terrorism
for a long time

2.
as a teen read pieces of the rise and fall
of the 3rd reich
not much more than a footnote
the points on jewish flesh stretched into lampshades
which, as it happened, echoed the fate of
slave rebellion leader nat turner a hundred years earlier
when his lush hued skin was cut and dried
and then fashioned into a purse and
a never quite translucent lamp shade
displayed in his captor's home
i've been against terrorism
for a long time

stood and marched
as vietnam warriors
would come and go leaving
chemical forests, massive graves
and skulls presaging
cambodian death trails

one half a million
iraqi children are dead
the first from poisoned water
then more from disease
and starvation
every thirty days
thirty-five hundred young people waste away
as if someone was blowing up
a child-full world trade center
inside of iraq every single month

and now america cries
speaks mournfully of mothers
who could not come home from work
fathers who had houses and dreams
turned to bone ash that got caught in our
phlegm-fill lungs and tear-spilling eyes
and yes we cry
for the loses of all of those
who were loved
who are loved
who are bombed
who were incinerated
who came to rest under hundreds of tons
of concrete and iron
plaster and glass
in barbarous acts
like so many others
that i have lived under
that i have seen grow

terrorism that's personal
a man dragged behind a truck
until his arm is pulled from socket
his leg torn from hip
his head sawed from neck

terrorism that's intimate
a woman raped invaded assaulted beaten
bruised broken by men
strangers and lovers
family every two minutes

terrorism that's official
a night stick pushed up a black man's anus
as a station full of police turn their heads
ignore the screams
a west african immigrant shot at 42 times
until 19 bullets make him
crumbles in his own doorway
while trying to show his papers

terrorism that's global

i have lost my mother my father
my brother my sister my hope
i have lost my family
so i have lost my hope
cries a man who speaks
after the bombing of his
afghani village
as the terrorists advance
boldly waving their flags

4.
america i hear you sing that
liberty is your mother
is it daddy then who rapes
because america
it is you who feeds

this monster its largest meals
you who stokes its hottest fires

no
you are not alone
and no
you were not the first
but now america you
set the standard

look at the people you have killed
start anywhere in your history
any day
the first days
this morning
spin a globe in your hand
and look where your armies live
look where they draw weapons
look where their armaments are used

but as for this american-born woman
grown strong and free inside
your rotting belly
america
terrorism has been a regular part of my world
all my life and i have been fighting it
long as i can remember
saying no as loud as i knew how

no pledges needed
no waving flags required
no uniformed allegiance
recited with bandaged mouths
necks gripped
until one can barely breathe

let me state it clearly again and again
i've been against terrorism
for a long time

been
against terrorism
against all terrorism

against terrorism
against all terrorism

against terrorism
against all terrorism for forever

— *devorah major*

THE TWIN TOWERS ARCANE

1.
Such mourning as we
might wake from
(having been woken from by such a light)
to see the light
at last:

that we are now
no more
nor less
   but have been more than others

a violent land

in our money markets
in our law 'n' orders
in our daily Dailies
in our beds

a violent life

pretending to an impenetrable innocence
and power symbolized
by those giant
Twins.

Their destruction:
Hitler's dream, dreamed before
they even were built,
before his suicide
began to fight on the side
of religious fanaticism.

And we
who had inherited so much
of his violence and anti-communism,
we who've even ultimately
financed the attack
on our pretended innocence

—we so at home
with fascism (denied, of course)
with brutality (foresworn, of course)
with liberty sentimentalized
from a core of destructive emptiness,
hopelessness,
cynicism at bottom,

children of a star-spangled
nihilism (of course denied and foresworn)

"from California
to the New York island"

brothers and sisters,
my own
so sadly struck,
so deeply struck.

2.
The Israeli says: "Now they know"
who himself has been infested
with genes
from the 12 year
long syringe of unforgettable evil.

Presumably it's we who now know
what it means to be totally detested
to the point of apocalypse.

And it's a fascist defense against
a fascist attack that the world
is preparing, for there's nothing
but that nothingness
of a scorpion planet eating
its own tail;

and it's the awareness of that truth
that doubles the mourning
and profounds the fear
of the loss of the innocence
that was a lie in the first place.

This time we're really trapped
by truth and it grieves us
who've been so comfortable
in the liberty of the lie.

This time the total mobilization
of war consciousness says:
even if pacifism grows,
even if it prevents responsive attacks,
even if non-violence triumphs,
the future will be
like a black man who,
or like eroticism which,
while no longer lynched or censored,
will nevertheless never
feel altogether at home
in worldly life.

The rule of nothingness
is complete now.
God murdered on one hand.
God suicided on the other.

The triumph of fascism.

We're ordered to live out
our non-violent lives
buying and selling
and praying to violence
despite ourselves

because there's nothing else,
nothing's changed,
it's only standing more revealed.

3.
Celia,
I know you ran toward
not away from,
to help, to save.

And that you saw the
second plane evaporate
in the wall as you ran
toward.

And that you saw, for
the first time in your life,
human beings leaping
from the high ledges.

and the Twins collapsing
into a single mountain
of thousand-fold death
and rubble and dust.

Nothing I was witness to
on a television screen
thousands of miles away
on another continent

can approach the horror
of what you saw as you
ran toward the scene
till you could no more,

dust-clouds billowing
through the streets and
those running for their
lives from the core

told you you could go
no further, couldn't help,
couldn't save, O my
brave, brave daughter.

I know your grief isn't
from afar. In vain, in vain
they died! you cry and
your despair there perhaps

spares, perhaps even saves
us from the shock which

turned the future into an
archaic archeological dig.

4.
The night that has arrived, the technological night, all day,
and with it mourning,
the fast of the fast,
the bitter taste
of one's own desert.

And that it is not only one's own
but that we're all speaking with mouths of sand,
and dunes are growing, undulating with the discourse
of a dazzling darkness in the sun
that is broken in each of us.

All night, airplanes and helicopters have been flying over
the burnt-sienna porticos of Bologna,
where I happen to be
mourning.
It's become the State
of Being.

A black flag
at half mast.

Hanging in mid-air.

— *Jack Hirschman*

THE MEETING OF THE POET
AND THE PRESIDENT

There is a passage in *Specimen Days*, August 12, 1863; here
it is August 12, 2001, a hundred and thirty-eight years
later, not so long. From his upstairs room near Vermont and
L in Washington the poet tells of seeing the president every
morning riding in to the White House from where he spends
the night, for the coolness, at a soldiers' home three miles
north of the city.

"I saw him this morning about eight-thirty. He always has a
company of twenty-five or so cavalry, with sabres drawn and
rides a good-sized, easy-going grey horse, is dressed in
plain black, somewhat rusty and dusty, wears a stiff black
hat and looks about as ordinary in attire as the commonest
man. I see very plainly Abraham Lincoln's dark brown face
with the deep-cut lines, the eyes, always to me with a
latent sadness. We have got so that we exchange bows, and
very cordial ones."

Sometimes one of his sons, a boy of eleven or twelve,
accompanies him, riding at his right on a pony. "They
passed me once very close, and I saw the president in the face
fully; his look, though abstracted, happen'd to be
directed steadily in my eye. he bowed and smiled, but far
beneath his smile I noticed well the expression I have
alluded to."

Lincoln's grief-eyes meeting Whitman's joy and wondering has
a great range of palette in the mix. The paint smears to
muddy rose with yellow streaks and polkadots of grey-green,
cobalt. Whitman's exuberant, always erotic, watching, the
wisdom of his excess: Lincoln's kind, saturnine, slightly
tickled, grin. Those days before cars, electricity, August
air-conditioning, and, seemingly with the polished sabres,
before guns, but not. There was the horrible, point-blank,
head-removing cannonfire going on, and these two bowing
faces, stupified with the events coming toward them, the boy

on the pony stunned from the photograph. I don't deny
there's goodness in this country, along with a fierce and
foolish pride, and some innocently cold determination, like
those horses in Whitman's journal stamping as they're being
unsaddled. Now led three at a time to a watering trough,
the wit of their tails flicking blackflies.

— *Coleman Barks*

ON CROSSING BROOKLYN FERRY, SEPTEMBER 11, 2001

1

I am with you, Walt Whitman
   on crossing Brooklyn Ferry face to face with Manhattan
sky
and you, Allen Ginsberg and Jack Kerouac
   on the road from park to pad to bar to Bellevue to
museum
   to the Brooklyn Bridge yacketayakking, screaming,
vomiting,
   whispering facts and singing songs of demons and
death—
WE the PEOPLE

I am with you, anonymous penthouser
   on balcony videotaping Boeing Jet slamming into 110-
floor Twin Tower
   and erupting into fireball of flame and billowing black
smoke
and you the female and male companions
   near camcorder screaming, "OMIGOD"
   and "HOLY FUCKIN' JESUS"—
WE the PEOPLE

I am with you, Lucy,
   on your last day of work at Aon Research
   in 105th floor Twin Tower office
and you, Jason,
   losing your mother on first day of school—
WE the PEOPLE

I am with you, Peter,
   huddling with Cantor Fitzgerald co-workers on 104th
floor
and you, Debbie,
   grieving for the securities trader fiance you were going

to marry
    this November —
WE the PEOPLE

I am with you, Michael,
    in 92nd floor studio working on life-size human figure
    about to take off in bronze flight "away from what is
repressive
    and toward what is redeeming"
and you, grieving Jamaican relatives
    and artist brothers and sisters throughout New York, the
USA,
    earth and Milky Way waiting to see his sculpture fly—
WE the PEOPLE

I am with you, angelheaded proletariat
    jumping from high windows like Mayan maids hurled
from edge
    of Chichen Itza cenote as sacrifice to rain god, Chac
and you, Steve,
    fleeing from debris raining from collapsing building as
Vesuvian ember
    and ashes upon terrified Pompeii residents–
WE the PEOPLE

I am with you, Genelle
    trapped in the rubble for 27 hours before you are pulled
out—
    the fifth and last person to be rescued
and you, her girlfriend,
    who held her hand while walking down the stairs from
the 64th floor
    of Tower Two and is still missing—
WE the PEOPLE

I am with you, emerging LA urban poet
    and artist wife discussing dissolution of 34 year bond
and trying to contact
    son who teaches art at Bronx high school

and you, Mark,
    returning call with shaky voice on cell phone while
walking on Brooklyn
    Bridge as you try to describe flames and smoke
ascending above
    starless dynamo in Manhattan machinery of night—
WE the PEOPLE

I am with you, woman folded in half
    with thigh missing on one leg and no foot on the other
    and you, volunteers
    gingerly placing each body part in separate bags—
WE the PEOPLE

2

I see Emma Lazarus
    wandering through crushed vehicles and shoes, purses,
umbrellas
    and baby carriages searching for glimpse of the Statue
of Liberty
and multi-cultural angels
    staggering on collapsed tower roofs illuminated,
    then descending with gas masks and 30,000 body bags
into the Pit
    searching for corpses and body parts of 5000 missing
New Yorkers—
WE the PEOPLE

I see holy Mayor Giuliani
    emerging from a cloud of smoke and dust with gray suit
    covered with ash
and Walt Whitman
    walking among the wounded in triage centers, stopping
here
    to dress a crushed head or there to undo the clotted lint,
remove
    the slough and wash off the matter and blood—
WE the PEOPLE

I see American flags
    flying from the redwood forest to the New York island
    on staffs mounted on auto windows
and thousands of candle light points
    streaming solemnly to twilights last gleam vigils in
response to calls issued
    from churches, synagogues, Buddhist temples and
Islamic centers—
WE the PEOPLE

                                3

I hear Palestinians
    from West Bank town of Nablus rejoicing and chanting
    "GOD IS GREAT!"
and Bill O'Reilly on Fox News Channel
    say that unless the Taliban quickly hands over Osama
bin Laden, "the U.S.
    should bomb the Afghan infrastructure to rubble — the
airport, the power
    plants, their water facilities and the roads. . . We should
not target civilians
    but if they don't rise up against this criminal
government, they starve, period."
WE the PEOPLE

I hear Nathan Baxter,
    Dean of the Washington Cathedral pray that as we
respond to this outrage
    "we don't become the evil we deplore."
and President Bush
    say at memorial service for victims "Americans do not
yet have
    the distance of history, but our responsibility to history
is already clear:
    to answer these attacks and rid the world of evil" —
WE the PEOPLE

I hear shots in Dallas
    and Waqar, Pakistani part owner of Mom's Grocery
Store lies dead
    then in San Gabriel, California
    and Adel Egyptian Coptic Christian owner of
International Market dies
    and leaves behind a wife and three children—
WE the PEOPLE

I hear in subway terminal
    while waiting for A-train Coltrane's eli eli lamma
lamma
    sabacthani saxophone cry
    followed by "Love Supreme" psalm
and Ginsberg in love bead necklace
    sitting cross legged, chanting Mahayana mantras
    invoking the deities of Mohandas Gandhi and Martin
Luther King
    to somehow overcome with good
    an ancient god of hellfire vengeance thirsty still
    for more human sacrificial blood—
WE the PEOPLE

— Carl Stilwell

NOTES TOWARD A POEM OF REVOLUTION

> *It is better to lose and win*
> *than win and be defeated.*
> —*Gertrude Stein*

1.
What did we in all honesty expect?
That fascist architecture flaunting
    @ the sky
converted now to fluid
    toxic
smoke,   ASH
the long finger of
                impermanence
touches us all   & nobody
can hog the marbles & expect
the others to play

2.
While we mourn & rant for years
over our 3000   how many
              starve
thanks to our greed
        our unappeasable
hunger

3.
WATER is rising
WIND is blowing

gonna strip the last of
             our
cheap & awkward
cities

only the music
some of the music
remains

4.
voice of my daughter
quivering on the phone
as she watches
the towers burn

from her new apartment
the one w/ the view. . .

5.
Gulf War, '91, my son
          @ the demonstration
stops by
          to eat

Well, we took out
a recruiting station
he tells me
while the cops
followed the crowd downtown
a group of us
split off.

          I nod &
bite my tongue.   Why talk about
what happened the year he was born?

6.
Wanted a northwest passage
& you've got it, Magellan!
Henry Hudson, A-mer-eee-go,
Da Gama,   are you proud
                    all of you
it took us
only 500 years to melt
that Polar ice

7.
And is it suicide when penguins
give up?   Lie down

8.
Children sold in Africa
in India
child labor laws held barely
eighty years,   now
eight year olds in brothels   dead
eyes
          who invented
this hell?

9.
Black holes in our hearts
ground zero
          our minds   hands
that won't open   let
                              go

10.
Tell me again how many janitors
died in the Towers
                    how many
                         sandwich makers'
toilet cleaners'
          families will get that
two-million-per-victim
          in aid?

11.
lost Montségur, we did
lost Prague,   the German
peasant uprisings   lost

Andalusia   (twice)
the Paris Commune

lost @ Haymarket
            lost
Paul Robeson   Spain
even lost   Dashiell Hammett

lost San Francisco   fairly
recently

12.
Chuck in his shorts
watering his garden

gunned down in the Mill Valley dawn

13.
we hole up
enclaves who speak
(again)   in whispers

as they did
when I first came
to these cities

14.
don't mourn
don't organize

strike & move on

— *Diane di Prima*

THE WAR

The War had its grandchildren over for the afternoon
they looked at the scrapbook
smiled, told one another jokes, ate well...
The War told everyone it was going to wear brand new clothes
but if you look close enough
the labels are angrily familiar...
The War knows where to buy food cheap
but good stuff nonetheless...
The War had a drinking problem
but it got smart, joined AA
nothing but coffee now...
The War came over to my apartment this afternoon
to borrow a video
I don't know as I should loan the War any of my things
It usually loses them, forgets to return anything...
The War got on its knees and prayed for more victims
before turning in.
Dear God, the War said, please let me go on and on and on
I am enjoying myself.
The War is getting younger all the time.
Nobody should look that young.
Nobody.

— *Scott Wannberg*

TOWERS DOWN

I am crying.
I am putting on a black shirt.
I am sorry for the lost lives.
I am celebrating.
It is not enough.

World Trade Center Towers:
down.
      Around town those
towers filled the windows.

Now: blue sky
and a wisp of smoke.

If they don't stay down
there's more needs be done.

Two towers: two strokes
on the dollar sign,
"S" the wavy course
planes took for impact.

The attack's on corporate greed,
not freedom. On the bottom line
running global companies
running the globe:
15% profit, 10% expansion.

Yellow-skin children glue
soles on our shoes.
Flowers suck water from a
brown family's vegetables.
TV's chemicals soak
a black family's soil.

Millions of families
grind dirt paying their
country's IMF debt.

I'm not running across

floor 79 and banging on
a door that won't open.

I am putting on a black shirt.
I am celebrating.
I am sorry for the lost lives.
I am crying.
It is not enough.

With no regard for human life
cowardly attackers slouch
behind logos and trademarks.

Money equals time equals
drudgery equals blood.

Line up for your vouchers,
your rice and beans, your
no time to watch the sun
set on how you once lived.

Buckle up at the sweat bench
and if you won't work
with the program, here come
the company assassins.

Shell in Nigeria,
United Fruit in Nicaragua,
Nike in the Philippines,
venture capital in Borneo.

Stand up and buck and they'll
roll out the carpet, red,
white, and blue. Unfurling
a gunship and tanks and the DOA
and a fat wad of greenbacks
stuffed in the colonel's pocket.

It's boring to list the abuses.

The Towers are down.
What they signify

I've hated since they
went up, and before them
the Empire State Building.

If they don't stay down
there's more to be done.

Now: blue sky
and a wisp of smoke.

I'm not running on floor 79
toward the windows while a
fireball warps the ceiling.

I am putting on a black arm band.
I am sorry for the lost lives.
I am celebrating.
I am crying.
It is not enough.

Let us never forget
the 3,000 dead.

Let us never forget
the 50,000,000 dead
since 1950 by the US
indirectly and directly.

Chile, Vietnam, Beograd,
Indonesia, Baghdad,
carpet bombing Cambodia.

It's boring to list the abuses.
Nagasaki, Somalia, Palestine.

It's horrifying to list
how many problems could've been
solved without bloodshed.

The carrot: buy this soft drink
and feel fine and feed
coins to the Towers.

The stick: rebel and lose
loans and get poorer and get
hungrier and get bombed.

The Pentagon is breached.
One fifth gone no balance
for those bent under its
gunmetal thumb worldwide
or put under the ground.

Money equals blood.
Blood invites retaliation.
Violence does not work.

Cemented with blood,
tiled with blood,
varnished with blood:
the Pentagon.
No longer invulnerable.

Today the engines are
quiet. Blue sky
and a wisp of smoke.

Let us never forget
the 3,000 dead.
Let us never forget
the 50,000,000 dead.

I'm not gasping on floor 79
breaking a window while
fiery air singes my lungs.

I am sorry for the lost lives.
I am crying.
I am celebrating.
I am putting on a black arm band.
It is not enough.

Let people create
their own cultures.

I want my regular M&Ms
not warped by 15%, 10%,
not crunchy, mini-bite, halloween.

My mailbox stuffed,
phone rung, TV dunned
with drums for war, for
buying, for war, for buying,
buying, buying, buying.
Buying bends in the walls.

Soon the FBI will punch
a microphone through the ceiling
to assess how much

I like this. I don't.

I'm not with you, 15%, 10%.
I'm not with you, military.
I'm not with you, Mr. President.

I'm against you.

You don't need
my fucking tax dollar
to buy a fucking microphone.

You have on boots
under which most
of the world writhes.
Give back the oil and money
and land and lives.

The Towers fall.
Earth heaves a sigh.
The sky rains gray.
It is not enough.

What my words could
not do, what Pacifica
could not do: done.

How wonderful! Finally

we live in the same
fear we create.

I am sorry for the lost lives.
I am celebrating.
I am crying.
I am putting on a black arm band.
It is not enough.

World Trade Center Towers
go down in a beautiful
orange and gray rasta do
growing a plume.

I'm not swinging from a flagpole
over a thousand-foot drop
with a firestorm behind me.

I'm not one of thousands
who dealt with horror in last
seconds and then horror
dealt with them.

You want others to feel that?
You want to retaliate?

You haven't noticed
the heart wrench?
How nothing can ease it?
Nothing.

You want revenge?
You want others to feel this?
They already do.
That's why this atrocity.

250,000 dead Iraqi children
from sanctions, Israeli bullets
wrapped in our dollars,
millions of our children
without health care.

Boring to list the abuses.

How awful for innocents to die.
How important the Towers have fallen.
How pivotal the Pentagon's breached.

I walk on ebullient feet.

The hammerlock loosens.
Symbols lose their grip.
Pentagon and Towers used to
key down corners of our minds.
Now the puzzle can unlock.

Now sky and sun can shine
on the human family
underneath 15%, 10%.

Sun and sky, open
a foundation of common feeling.
Blue sky
and a wisp of smoke.

If they don't stay down,
there's more needs be done.

Let us never forget
the 3,000 dead.
Let us never forget
the 50,000,000 dead.

Take responsibility.

Walk the street
on ebullient feet and scan
faces for kindred hope.

Singing and dancing ahead,
young people celebrating
young lust, hips and sneakers
tilting over untouched sidewalk.

Not on the streets

of Lower Manhattan, not
slogging through rubble
two feet deep concealing
the dead and the half alive.

Not slogging through ashes
two feet deep hiding

clasped hands, black and white;
clasped hands, old and young;
clasped hands, rich and poor.

I am crying.
I am crying.

It is not enough.

— *Clive Matson*

SEPTEMBER 12

I.

We had this language down there.
Words re-invented, new to their skins.
The Pile, we said, *The Dust* and *The Hole*,
Liberty One, Tower Two, The Millennium.
Everyone needed a *Mask* and a *Hat.* Longed for fresh *Socks.*
And these words that we knew, that we'd already known,
became foreign, and special, and harsh on the tongue.

II.

Small red bag,
almost hidden in the corner
of the dim, crowded room.

Label:
Female, Thirties
Left arm,
Wedding Band.

III.

The noise was a constant screech and bang
thud. Creak of cranes, scrape of tires. Beeps
when the trucks backed up over the crushed curbs, and
the crunch of charred paper under your feet. It was constant,
uneven; after a while you stopped bothering to hear.

You knew it was bad when the rhythm began.
Before you heard words you heard thumping,
a heartbeat, a swelling of drums as hard boots
thundered towards you. *Run run run*
Go go go Get out of here guys
ditch the supplies just run go go run

as the skyscraper bent,
willow-sweet overhead.

IV.

A duck walked into a bar.

A bear walked into a bar.

A firefighter walked into a bar.
Then the whole place caved in on him.

V.

Movie on Mute:

Two men in turnout coats holding a stretcher
draped with red plastic. Lumpy.

They're in a garage, surrounded by gurneys.
Behind them, shelves filled with

bandages, saline, betadine, alcohol,
scissors, splints, tubing, C-collars.

Back to the men. They're filthy and tired,
trading words with a woman who points back at the door.

Turn on the Sound:

This is East Triage. The morgue is in Liberty One.

"Not anymore. Liberty One's coming down,
the National Guard has gone in to pull out
all the bodies. They said this is the place now."

This isn't the place. Trust me, guys.

"Well, what are we supposed to do with this?"

Turn on the Smell:

Turn it off, turn it off.

I don't know.

VI.

On a night two months later I found,
in a dream, two stones
in my jacket pockets. I told them
I'd give them the names Through and Storm.
Then a voice from everywhere said No,
their names are White and Hound. Meanwhile
silver train cars plummeting
from the night sky, lethal
as stars.

— *Cory Ellen Nadel*

I DON'T KNOW
Jalal, Age 48   Yemen

When I hear the whistle for work
I take my coffee
And go to take my gloves
See Mr. Tim what I work on today
He say complete the job from yesterday
I start to work
I'm working 20 minutes
a half hour
and he say to me
Don't work. Go home
I tell him why I go home?
He say
You are Arabic
You are Muslim
You don't see what happened in New York
Washington?
You don't see how many people
your people killed?

I tell him I not do nothing. I work here.
I have been here fifteen years
How can I go home?

He say Go pray in your mosque
Go pray with your leader I
don't want you to work here.

For half a minute
or a minute I'm thinking what can I do?

He say, "If you don't go, I get the
police for you."
I hear that he say
Maybe there is trouble
So I go
I have my check coming the next day

But I don't go get it I'm too scared
I think maybe if I go there
he do something I
don't know.

— *Michael McLaughlin*

PEACE STUDIES AT THE RHODE ISLAND AVENUE BARBERSHOP

People running round in circles, don't know what they headed for,
everybody crying peace on earth, just as soon as we win this war."
—*Mose Allison*

It comes as a great shock around the age of five, six, or seven to discover
that the flag to which you have pledged allegiance...has not pledged
allegiance to you...
—*James Baldwin*

no flags fly in this shop
barber spriggs, whose family was run out of
jackson, ms. in '56 for registering voters,
refuses to allow opportunistic jingoists to
thump their chests in this moment of mourning,
says simply, "no flags"

he doesn't mention what the whole shop knows,
has sent two sons to the gulf:
one came back broken, with dreams
he could not end by waking,
the other suffers from a disease that
the govt. swears he does not have

instead he says,
"this ain't the time for flag wavin'
time for thinkin beyond killin' & revenge,
beyond causes & countries
i'm ready for some peace"

more eloquent than hitchens or chomsky
i put my copy of the nation down
listen, while in the background al green croons
willie nelson's, "Time Slips Away"

scissors scrap across faded hair
create a percussive snip
like wire brushes on high hat
as the unreconciled racist past
comes as muted testimony from mr. spriggs

"but we is americans, goddamnit"
someone asserts, stating the obvious
like the insistent prayer of a faithful sinner
like this ain't suppose to be happenin — to us

"shit was horrific, & dem bastards
need dey ass kicked..." begins barber spriggs
hands smelling of coconut spray & alcohol,
"but by the same token," a barbershop preamble,
to getting your hole card pulled,
"you know what they say,
ya keep running roun' world
stickin' yo dick in other people's beehives
ya gotta expect to get stung"

put the pundits to sleep
let the political hacks go home
its all been said now,
no commercial interruptions
for the sale of american flags
with made in china labels

the quiet hum of clippers
& nappy hair falling to
black & white floors
the gallery nods in agreement
no one calls it karma
or speaks of chickens returning to roost

what these black men know this Saturday
is that the same ol, same ol
will not save us now
battle hymns & cacophonous anthems

are no substitute for justice or peace

when it is my turn
barber spriggs steps outside
snaps the apron in well worn ritual
it sounds like a flag whipping in the Sept. breeze
it even has red & white stripes

but it has never been to war
never waved to mock the democracy it represents
never decorated a flag pole used
to lance a black man in boston

i salute the apron in an anti-ritual
for the innocent dead
& the innocent dead to come
i note its absence of stars

the man with the bag of american
flags noiselessly disappears,
like clumps of black hair
blown by a wayward western wind.

— *Kenneth Carroll*

THE FALLEN TOWER - SEPTEMBER 11, 2001

Images indelibly burned
into the silver coated mind.
Planes flying into towers,
erotic symbols of power and wealth.
The towers falling in upon themselves
like a person slowly kneeling
in submission to a divine will.
But inside the debris
lie the crushed and torn bodies
of 3000 workers. Their dreams
and their futures terminated.
Their loved ones walking aimlessly
around lower Manhattan holding
the pictures of their lost loves
bled from their computer printers.
Three thousand lines of future history
sucked into death's black hole.

Words merely describing the images
spreading a dread into the light
while darkness remains adorned
by the ominous moon
and its necklace of stars.

The vast world encircling
web America has secured
to the four directions
is now shattered and torn.
The threads of our security,
our wealth, and enormous power
are ruptured and we will try
to repair the emptiness
and fill it with the marching bands
of military might and righteous anger

The spider will flail and destroy and injure
the guilty and the innocent

and more enemies will find
new ways to blind Cyclops
and defeat Goliath with a slingshot.

We are the leaders.
We who care about all life.
We who imagine a shared humanity
on a lonely planet floating through the heavens.
We who care about our endangered future.
We who are disheartened
about our enormous appetite
exploiting peoples all over the world.
We who want an end to oil politics
and to begin a new era based
on the natural energies
the creation has provided us.
We who need to live
for the well being of all.
We to whom the saints taught
of love and compassion.
We to whom the martyrs in those
crushed buildings and the fiery jets,
their ghosts hovering in our hearts,
have called not to revenge
but to a new crusade
of reconciliation between nations,
between the rich and poor
between humanity and nature
between the present
and our children's future.

— *Allen Cohen*

WHATEVER HAPPENED
TO THE AGE OF AQUARIUS?
APRIL 23, 2002

Yet another birthday
to acknowledge the passage of time
and the hope of immortality,
that harbors the dream of death
and crystallizes the memory of never dying
like the California Indians,
who had few tools and weapons
and were thought to be primitive
yet performed a six day ceremony to aid
the soul on its journey to the other world.

This year as a new love resurrects my soul
we have seen our country and the world
tie itself in knots of confusion and corruption.
As we move into the 21st Century
the American world empire
has fallen into chaos
with the fool on the hill
turning his back on a world
that needs to move toward unity and justice.

We have been attacked
like Goliath blinded by David
and Polyphemus blinded by Ulysses.
America is the one eyed son of the sea god
and gluttonous earth eater
that is without concern for the world
it must care for and depend upon.

With the sea rising
and the ice melting
the corruption and scandal
rise to the surface.
The towers of commerce collapse
from the blow of a sling shot

and the fire of the eye blinding torch.
Corporations run naked in the streets
of their greed and shame.

The hypocritical life denying church
revealed as hypocrites in their suppression
of human sexual need as guiltlessly
for centuries the priests, cardinals
and bishops have raped children.

In Bethlehem where the child of compassion,
forgiveness and non-violence was born,
Moslem warriors hide out
and are surrounded by Jewish tanks
in a siege that can only end
by a surrender to the principals
of the child born in the barn
that stood there 2000 years ago.

The universe once thought of as an empty void
is now seen as a fertile ocean
of creations and annihilations.
Our planet with its wondrous oneness
of interactive forms and processes
is spinning through the dark sea
as the human species crosses
the threshold of evolutionary potential —
of barbarism and extinction,
or an exhilaration of compassion and forgiveness.
We must make the leap from empire to love.

—*Allen Cohen*

COME REST WITH ME, O LORD

Come rest with me, O Lord!
Before you go down
that awful road.
You must be weary
of all the prayers
reeking of revenge
and bloody reprisal,
each prayer plowing
another furrow
on your infinitely
wrinkled brow.

Do not be angry
as all these bodies
you so delicately
cultivated through
millions of years
fall wounded and
dying at your feet.
Each one reaching
toward that long sought
embrace with the idea
of perfect union.

Come rest with me
upon this soft pillow
before you venture out
to the battlefield of archaic
hate and fear and loneliness
that tears your flesh
upon the cross of knowing!

You have given us the choice
of destruction or unity
but we continually choose
to destroy as we inch
toward the prophesied end.

The wars and wounded multiply
and the nuclear genie
is out of the bottle again.
The human world
spins chaotically forgetting
your enormous and
ecstatic presence within us.
Come rest here with me!
Let me sooth your wounds
and grave disappointments
before you go down
that dreadful road again.

I want to be your lover, dear one,
Come rest in my arms
beneath my warm covers!
Then in the dawn we will
rise again renewed!

You have warned us
us of the wars and plagues
as we tear each other apart
just to claim your name.
You knew the wounds and cuts
would pierce your body
as we become obsessed
by the idea of separation.

Come rest with me!
I will keep you warm
here beside me
in this long bitter night.
I know the time
to choose has come.
The message sketched
like a treasure map.
in our genes.

We have placed an eye

in the heavens to see
the moment of creation.
Yet we destroy ourselves
on the battlefields
murdering for your love.

Come rest with me!
You need to be embraced
and comforted before daybreak
as the time for healing
or for destruction ascends
through our wounded hearts
onto the verdant fields
of transcendent history.

— *Allen Cohen*

10:45 A.M. SEPT. 11/WTC

whywhywhy.....whywhywhy
whywhywhy.....whywhywhy
whywhywhy.....whywhywhy
whywhywhy.....whywhywhy
whywhywhy.....whywhywhy
whywhywhy.....whywhywhy
whywhywhy.....whywhywhy
whywhywhy.....whywhywhy
whywhywhy.....whywhywhy
whywhywhy.....whywhywhy
whywhywhy.....whywhywhy
whywhywhy.....whywhywhy
whywhywhy.....whywhywhy
whywhywhy.....whywhywhy
whywhywhy.....whywhywhy
whywhywhy.....whywhywhy..............whywhywhy
whywhywhy.....whywhywhy ....whywhy..why..why
whywhywhy.....whywhywhy......whywhy.whywhywhywhy
whywhywhy.....whywhywhy.. whywhywhywhy..whywhywhywhy
whywhywhy.....whywhywhy..whywhywhywhywhywhywhywhywhywhywhy?

— *Mark Kuhar*

ON A ROADSIDE IN OHIO

the sign on interstate 271, right there,
says new york: hundreds of miles
up the highway, why it mentions new york
on a roadside in Ohio is beyond me.
i've been living in the wretched dark,
is it safe to come out now? my muse
has been blown to bits, my words buried
beneath the rubble like 3,000 ended lives.
i look into the eyes of people who walk
past me & i see either fear or a plot
10 years in the works, a knowing smile,
a wink that asks me if i'm in or if i'm out.
i'm way out, fled to stone caves in the green
woods, where carved stone faces of stern lions
clipper ships, ty cobb, loom above me
like ancient stained glass in a cathedral.
i'm trying to absorb all of this, seek
the meaning of things that are undefined,
ask the questions that have no reply.
at night sometimes i hear a baby cry,
not sure if it's my son or a spirit wavelength.
today i saw exhaust trails airplaned across
the bluest of skies, a question mark cloud,
a path that leads to wherever metal flies.
i feel like i live in an armed prison camp.
i've seen tanks roll away from the airport,
military jets buzz through the twilight.
tonight baseball games are being played,
sandlot sluggers like a warm wool blanket.
there is comfort in the familiar, quiet
in my heart broken only by echoes of last week's
news reports, ticker runners, vile footage.
over the internet prayers, replies, sabre rattling.
i am drained from white light slowed
to a trickle, i feel like i may be the only thing
holding the earth on its axis & that's funny.
do you know what i want to do? i want

to take you in my arms and spend a thousand
hours making love to you, replicating
the expression of pure emotion, procreating
miniature fireballs of expanded healing,
atoms that split and multiply until the universe
is drowning in a torrent of love, peace
acceptance, beauty, brotherhood, flowing
waves of timeless safety & sweet security
that circles the earth & the planets with
the speed of sound, godenergy fabricating
renewed worlds. i'm cracking the door
open tonight. are you out there? can you
hear me? & whatever you ask of me i will do,
on the tripping tempest of these frightened times

—*Mark Kuhar*

IF BIN LADEN READ DR. SEUSS

so then, bin laden, is this
what you do for fun? blow
people up? kill? destroy?
i have some suggestions
you might want to try instead.
read dr. seuss. smell a flower.
do a cartwheel. watch little
children playing & drink grape
kool aid. paint pictures with
red & green tempura. eat an
orange. bin laden, you have
four wives. doesn't sex do it
for you? open yr arms to the
smiling moonlight. tell yr
lieutenent to put down his gun
& the two of you play catch.
fire up some afghani red in
a 12-hose hookah & bliss out.
did you ever watch a bogart
movie? how about cartoons?
bin laden, allah is not honored
when you kill 3,000 americans.
feed three thousand with loaves
& fish & see what allah says
about that. dude, can't you go to
a soccer game or a chili joint?
feed pidgeons in the park?
bin laden millions of afghans
are starving, can't you use
yr millions to drill wells
& grow wheat? the arab world
needs a savior, not a fugitive killer.
you could build a band-aid factory
& manufacture penicillin &
piece together lost souls with
ointment & a gentle touch.
bin laden we look up at the same

sky, count the same stars, watch
vast oceans from the same precipice.
don't you get it, man? yr fever
can be measured in degrees.
we have but one mission: to
clothe the naked, build houses
for the homeless, carry the sick
to the doctor. not so very far from
where you are, mother teresa
reached out to the wretched
poorest of the poor in india's slums.
where did it all go wrong bin laden?
tonight you will dream of lambs
& flutes & calm nectars from
fruited vines, because i will it so
& that white light you see is my
shadow. open yr heart man, have
some green eggs, i know you don't
eat ham, & i'd like you to meet
my friend, his name is sam i am

—*Mark Kuhar*

LAST THOUGHTS 9/11 VOICES

all memories
are piled on the pyre
of history
this is no different

Woman I
i will not give up
i must Keep moving
how will they know
the cake is ordered and paid for
i did not forget
it was to have been a surprised
when i got home from work
fifteen years old and all we do now is fight
about his pants too big and hanging
his music blasting vulgar lyrics
lord spare me to tell him
i love you my only son
i love you

mercy
my body is on fire

the morning of the terror
is still too new
to reflect on the pleasure
of courtship and move beyond
victim someone
must be blamed
for this transgression

Fireman
i woke with a headache
my body felt used up
like a discarded toilet-paper roll
i could not have guessed
that i could work so long
so hard surrounded by smoke and ashes
the despair and bewilderment

in people's eyes
i'll never be able
to wash away
it's not easy to
find the truth
on this table
of politics and domination
everyone outside
of the closed conference rooms
is a pawn and a victim

Young Man
i don't believe in much
i don't know any god
but right now at this moment
i want to believe at least in liberty
smoke and ash blinding my eyes
i hope she knows i love her
that she is the first person i ever
loved that i had the ring
picked out that i'm sorry
about the affair

dignity and grace
seldom look as we imagine
and if we believe
as we often teach our children
two wrongs don't make a right
then how to explain
which terror
precipitated which terror
who are the innocent

West Indian Woman
lawd god look how me
come america fi betta me life
fi get weh from the violence
to come meet death this Tuesday morning
what go happen to me four
children who gwane look

afta dem no place fi run

charged emotions
is good to fuel
narrow nationalism
and random retaliation

Security Guard
i told my idiotic boss
after the first tower exploded
in flames
that we should evacuate
why didn't i listen to my
instincts i've got a wife
three children mortgage
i just paid for our first cruise
damn these crazy folks

you will remember
september 11
but remember too
all the days
when life was
routine and you swore
at someone for a slight infraction
and you neglected to tell
your children or mate
you love them
and you did not smile
at the person who walked right
by you and you complained
without gratitude

what will your
voice recall
if sudden death
claims you
live without regrets

— *Opal Palmer Adisa*

IT MUST NOT HAPPEN

My days like water. I clip the toenails
of the Great One. Follow strict orders to obey
him. Blurred hours of rinsing rice, endless fight
against dust. Bleat of goats outside. Drawn
to my husband's computer, not permitted
to touch it. Re-named "Nafira." I was
Stephanie, lived in Los Angeles. They call me
one of the Saved Ones, but every night I dream
of car keys, music, lipstick, movies, laughter and palm
trees. My new husband is patient with me. He knows I saw
buildings crumble, how thick smoke
nearly claimed me. I thought, this must
not happen. At times I feel

fire burn through me. It's when I walk
quietly towards the vegetable market,
with my chaperone. Or when I remember
my mother's shredding skin, don't understand
why my husband lies beside me.
What this has to do with God.
But I knew when I brought
the Great One soup, I could not kill him.
I saw the Towers in his eyes.
How silver cell phones, crumpled paper
fell from windows. My shoes.
My red dress. My cabinet
of denials. My innocence.
Where I once lived
there were so many prayer vigils.
I believed them.
I saw the Great One's purple robe,
his feet. I looked down, as instructed.
Not at his face.
I have become water.
Everything has burned away.
And even if I still believe
I'll wake up

tomorrow in my own bed,
in Los Angeles,
as I might, as you
still might, wherever
you are, know only this:
the bad dream
has entered us. We cannot
lose ourselves, go to meet it.
No more mass burials
by a harbor.

— *Sharon Olinka*

AFTER

When the towers fell
a conundrum;

Shall these from eternity
inherit the earth,
all debts amortised?

Gravity was ungracious,
a lateral blow
abetted, made an end.

They fell like Lucifer,
star of morning, our star
attraction, our access.

Nonetheless, a conundrum;
Did God approve, did they prosper us?

The towers fell,
money amortised in pockets
emptied, once for all.

Why did they fall, what law
violated? Did Mammon
mortise the money
that raised them high, Mammon
anchoring the towers in cloud,
highbrow neighbors
of gated heaven and God?

'Fallen, fallen is Babylon the great...
they see the smoke
arise as she burns...'

We made pilgrimage there.
Confusion of tongues.

Some cried vengeance.
Others paced slow, pondering

— this or that of humans drawn forth,
dismembered —.

a last day; Babylon
remembered.

— *Daniel Berrigan*

THE CATHOLIC BISHOPS APPROVE BUSH'S WAR

Lest I merge
with mountains that surely will fall,
their decrepitude my own —

Lest I walk shod
in blood of Abel, crying from the earth;
'My tantamount, my brother, my undoer' —

Lest eons I must carry
Rachel's sacrifice, her tears my albatross —

Lest I the Christ
disavow,
and Him who shackled there
I drag through sludge
of cowardice and dismay —

Lest weighed, I be found
wanting —
no guest of heaven,
a ghost, and no egress
from foolish trumpery of time —

Lest I disappear, down down
the 110th escalation
of pride,

and truncated, eyeless, soulless,
be found
unfit for armed might,
for rubble and America —

Lest I be sifted
like wheat or chaff,
and under a pall

(the appalling flag)

am borne away
piecemeal
to broken doorways
of shoel or limbo,

the divergencies
not large, nor mine to choose) —
Lest I

—*Daniel Berrigan*

WORLD TRADE CENTER

I am an old woman in a black dress
kneeling in the ruins, clutching my shoulders,
teeth clenched and lips drawn back in a snarl,
rocking back and forth in grief and rage.
I need to tear out my enemy's throat
for the taste of his lifeblood
is better than strawberries.
I am kneeling in the ruins of Byzantium.
I am kneeling in the ruins of New York.
I am saying the names of my dead children
over and over, as if they were silver bullets
to shoot at God's smile,
but I want to kill my enemy's children
more than I want my own children back.
My face is twisted and strong.
People in uniforms want me to stand up
and get out of their way.
I ignore them.
The sky's a pillar of smoke above me.
There "s a pillar of fire raging inside me.
I clench my shaking old hands into fists.
I need to squeeze my enemy's throat:
more than I need to hold my lover in the sweet and warm.
His body's in front of me, squashed to a bloody pulp
with fallen metal.
Somebody takes our picture.
I am kneeling in the ruins of Jerusalem.
I am kneeling in the ruins of Ireland.
I am kneeling in the ruins of New York.
I am kneeling in the ruins of Stonehenge
that was a city once.
This was a world once
and I was human once but I've forgotten it.
I walk on bloody feet thru war.
Dying soldiers kneel to me
and I smile.

— *Julia Vinograd*

JERUSALEM DURING A SUICIDE BOMBING

Jerusalem strolled thru an outdoor market
during a suicide bombing.
It rained fingers and oranges
and blood bright as summer cherries.
Strawberry ice cream cones blew straight up
and knocked birds off their course,
then fell back on a little boy's scabbed knee,
the rest of him was gone.
The wind of the blast blew
thru Jerusalem's prayers,
her hair roared back like a lion,
like 2 lions mating in mid-air.
Jerusalem's eyes half-closed,
her lips parted, gasping a little,
lost in the moment like any woman in a bed.
Ritual men with bags go thru the scene,
collecting body parts
to be buried together like jigsaw puzzles
but Jerusalem is a puzzle whose pieces change shape
when the wind blows.
She smiles and yawns,
her hills breathing like breast.
Jerusalem remembers when it rained frogs
and men fought in chariots
with swords for her
and died calling her name.
Feathers knocked off birds that don't care
wind up pressed between pages
of the Books of the law.
Jerusalem's naked feet leave the scene of love,
nothing changes.

— *Julia Vinograd*

TIME TO DIE　*SEPTEMBER 11, 2001*

He called to say he was stuck at work.
There was just no way
He could come home early today.
Maybe, he wouldn't come home at all.
It might be never.
He said, a little catastrophe
Has just happened to me,
And to all the people in the offices here
TODAY!
Bow your head and pray.
The ceiling is starting to cave in.
Out the window I see a fireman.
But, he can't get near.
There's too much fire and smoke in here.
I think we've been hit by a bomb.
God, I wish I could come home!
If I never see you again, I love you.
Yes, I know you love me too.
I'm busy now, Goodbye.
I'm sorry, I have to take time to die.

— *Karen Elizabeth Harlan*

CAVES, WAR, AND PEOPLE
(thanks to Glenn Gray, WW II)

"At ease,"
the young lieutenant barks at our rifle squad,
tired from a long march.
We are outside Da Nang.
"You, soldier," he points in my face.
"Yes, sir," I stiffen to attention.

"See that cave?"
"Yes, sir."
"Charlie's in there.
He's hiding.
Hunt him down.
Smoke him out."
"Yes, sir."

The last cave I entered,
looking for VC,
flashes in my mind.
I felt like a mole.
Poisonous snakes
might attack me.

Trapped in a small space,
unable to see very well.
I didn't want to go back
into another smelly tunnel.
What if the enemy set a trap?

"Come on out,"
we yelled.
"We know you're in there."
I had been in-country only a few days—
still a teen-ager,
playing games,
this boy solider.

We waited.
"Come on out."

We waited for what seemed like a long time.

Hearing no sound,
we assumed no one was inside.
So we finally threw a few firecracker grenades in,
counting them as they exploded—
one, two, three....
Yes! July 4th—explosions, a light show.

Expecting no one inside,
we edged in...
body parts everywhere....

We couldn't look at each other,
hung our heads in shame,
unable to say anything.

We needed a body count:
we tallied parts of seven small bodies...
and nine old, thin bodies of small-boned people.

That was a tiny cave.
This one is huge.

I take my flashlight and M16.
Now a seasoned veteran at the age of nineteen,
I'm on a manhunt into a cave again,
now carrying small-boned people inside me.

Each family has staked out a little space
in this dank dungeon.
The stench hits me first—
holes in the ground for excrement.
I gag,
want to throw up.
I'm trained, disciplined,
but not for this.

Acrid smoke hits my eyes—
small fires for light and cooking—
blinding this mole even more.

No wind, no ventilation, no water.
This is surely Hell.
How blind we are.

I stumble, grope forward,
try to avoid stepping on bodies.
Hundreds are lying, sitting, crouching—
children screaming,
old men and women coughing or moaning.
No men of fighting age, yet.

Far into the cave,
my head hits the ceiling
and I fall to my knees.

I throw out a hand,
touching not the filthy floor,
but the fingers and palm of a woman's hand,
raised to stop me from falling on her.
Our survivals are suddenly linked.

Is she the enemy?
Where am I?
What am I hunting?
Who is this woman?

I feel her grasp become a clasp—
sensuous, even amorous,
tracing the lifeline on my palm.
She traces the lifeline on my palm.

Unable to surrender to her feeling,
I release my hand,
mumble an apology,
and bolt out of the cave.
Outside, I hold my splitting head in my hands.

How could anyone experience desire in such a hellhole?

— *Shepherd Bliss*

HELD CAPTIVE

You come in on it early 5:48 PDT when
all the world's a sleeping machine and you
in your dreaming and you in your guilt
for work yet to be done hear the radio news
reader say it appears that a plane might have
crashed into the World Trade Center building
in New York then when you hear the man say
"No maybe two planes have crashed against
the Trade Center" you the rememberer lie
in bed playing back the time you and Janet went
to shop at Century 21 across from the Trade Center
where at the door you watched two young men
one Black the other Puerto Rican stop young
Blacks and Puerto Ricans and turn them away

"Prejudice prejudice" you cried and one of them
said "Hey these guys come in here and steal
and we know who it is does the stealing it's
the Blacks and Puerto Ricans and so I'm Black
and he's Puerto Rican so we're just doing our job
where you from anyway man just be cool"

And those are the thoughts those are dreams
that come floating back when you get out
of bed click into TV and see for yourself no
for your*selves* the smoke and flames then hear
the names called off Osama Bin Lauden
Afghanistan banana stand the secret code
in that movie with Zero Mostel but this is
no movie this is the real thing this is dingy dusty
destiny played out like roosting chickens like
what Malcolm X talked about and ended up
in trouble with the Nation of Islam then history
put the whammy on Elijah Muhammad and Malcolm
got X'ed and another lost age got scripted

This screenplay struggles and tugs at your heart

when in defense of dignity you pray they don't
go screaming Arab dirty Arab and pull the rug
out from under all your Arab American friends

— *Al Young*

THE EQUATION

Horrific towers of flame over Manhattan like nothing
so much as Hanoi in that first haze of rubble.
That rain of corpses much like the storm of death
we vomited over Quang Ngai, or Pyongyang
after Walker's 8th Army got through with the place.
Or Beirut, after Haig gave the nod to Sharon
and the Christian Phalange was let loose
on the refugee camps. Or the corpses
we planted all over Managua; the slaughter
that Kissinger's White House unleashed
on East Timor & Pinochet's Chile.
And always the same bloody equation:
Our lives matter; theirs are of no consequence whatsoever.
Now the Trade Center's gone.
Who'd have believed it? The air thick with some
sort of festering stench
as the innocent dead are stuffed into bags,
& Old Glory unfurls in the breeze.
Good Lord, what a fog
of feculent speeches! What a ghoulish intoxication!
The eagle sharpens her claws.
In the air a lust to spill somebody's blood.
Whose, at this point, doesn't much matter.
No doubt Baghdad will pay; the Afghans are toast.
They'll be blown away by the tens of thousands.
Guilty or not, it's gonna be open season. The Good
Ozymandian folk are waving their flags
& shrieking for blood.
Nationwide polls
have shown that it holds, no less today
than a thousand years in the past: that ancient
tribal equation: the massacre of a few hundred thousand
innocent souls won't cause but the shrug
of an indifferent shoulder,
a rhetorical tear or two of remorse
just so long,
of course,
as the mangled dead aren't our own.

— *Steve Kowit*

WILL BOLAND & I WALK DOWN THE BEACH

Seething over this filthy war that every chest-thumping
imbecile in the country's in love with, Will & I walk
from Dog Beach down to Cape May. Midwinter, dusk,
the coast all but deserted: a man walks his golden retriever;
a couple's out hunting for shells; two good old boys,
clutching their Michelobs take in the last of the sunset:
stuck in the sand at their feet, a gigantic American flag.
Tens of thousands of miles away, women crouch
in the rubble rocking their dead. "The world's
most malignant species," I grumble. Two high school
girls, wading in & out of the surf, smile up at us sweetly.
"Yes. But with all that, a magnificent world," Will
adds quietly. "& one that we're just as much a part of
as anything else." We walk a bit further in silence,
& stop. At our feet, the Pacific, ablaze in magentas & red.
"Maybe so," I concede. "...but the ugliest part.") The words
hardly out of my mouth when those two young women,
now some twenty yards down the beach, fling open their arms,
rise to their toes, & launch themselves into the dusk,
to alight in a gorgeous dazzle of pirouettes. Will & I
stand there. Grinning. Dumbfounded. Amazed. Under the flare
of the night's first stars, each exuberant leap more lofty, rapturous,
vaulting! Two splendid young ballerinas, silhouetted
against the indigo flames off the darkening Western horizon.
The last of the light of this world setting behind them.

— *Steve Kowit*

NOTHING IS THE SAME THE DAY AFTER

The Gathering

They are gathering in the blackness
That follows a tremendous wind,
Gathering in the spent fields of New York
And Washington, looking through
The loosened threads of light
That drift down from the hem of the sky.
It is the morning after.

They are gathering in the black smoke
Of the mangled, the singed, and the buried
searching the rubble of the once was,
searching for the buried living and the buried dead,
the people tossed down from the sky
like flaming rockets,
swan diving from the list of the living
They are searching for a man
With the tattoo of a whale (or a
dolphin) surrounded by a starfish
An office worker who loved raspy rock and roll
The woman who was a whiz in the kitchen
The one who had a passion for stylish shoes.

All of this would be easier if there were someone—
(Call him God)—to help—(call him Allah)
To find a fireman—(call him Jesus) or
A window washer—call him Yahweh
Or the mountain man who
Toppled from the 104th floor
(Call him the great spirit.)

All of this would be easier if they had the eyes
Of a beloved someone
(Call him Krishna)
The eyes of Allah
The eyes of God

— Ann Marie Samson

DIMINISHING RETURNS

In the Fall of 2001,
it seemed that sky and earth
collided and people rained down.

The rescuers began
by looking
for live bodies,
then dead bodies,
then body parts,
and finally,
DNA *samples*.

Home
went
the families
with urns
of dirt.

— *Charlotte McCaffrey*

NEWSPAPER

They manufacture newsprint with a grain,
So you can tear straight down a vertical column.
But if you try to tear it crosswise, it rips
Out of control, in jagged scallops and slashes,
Serrated chaos like the blocks of smoking ruin.
Here amid columns is a man who handles
Search dogs. He says the dogs depend on rewards.
But not like the dogs I know, not dog treats: the Lab
Who'll balance one on his muzzle, trembling and gazing
Up at you till you say "*okay!*" then he whips
It into the air and snaps it and bolts it whole.
No, what the handler says is that his dogs
Are trained to find survivors—that's their reward,
Finding somebody alive is what they want.
And when they try and try and never get it,
They get depressed, he says: "These dogs are depressed."
Yes, what an animal thing depression is,
The craving for some redemption is like a thirst.
It's in us as we open the morning paper:
Fresh, fallible, plausible. It says the smoke
Was mostly not paper or flesh. First white, the drywall,
Then darker pulverized steel and granite and marble,
And then, long-smoldering toxic plastic and fiber.
In the old days, the printing plant and "the paper"
(Meaning the Globe or Herald or Journal or Times)
Were in one building, and the tremendous rolls
Of newsprint tumbled off the trucks each day.
When I was small one crushed a newsboy's legs.
There was a fund for him, I remember his picture
Accepting a powered wheelchair or special crutches.
His name would be in the files of the Daily Record.
The one-way grain is like the irrevocable,
Downward river of time set into channels.
Words broadcast on the air don't seem as solid.
Paper—the bread of Chronos, titanic Time
That eats its children. And the crosswise jumble
That won't tear straight unless you cut it is like

Darkness innate in things. The weather. The boy
Who beams up at the camera or down at his stumps.
The prisoner who speaks an unknown language
So that their captors guess and call him "the Chechen."
The errant, granular pulp. In some old stories,
The servant rises early and reads it first,
Then gets the iron and presses it flat and smooth
To place by the master's breakfast—the skin of days.

— *Robert Pinsky*

THE 911 WAKEUP CALL

The special effects merchants have been humbled.
America has been sucker punched and the city that never sleeps
Is afraid to close its eyes.
The need for speed was eclipsed in the span of one hour with
The cessation of air-travel, cell phone service and the closing of
        Starbucks.
Rumors of Armageddon and the pending rapture sent sinners and
        saints
Scrambling for the comforting tones of Oprah and Graham
Of Giuliani and Rather, Ashcroft and Powell and finally the new and
        improved
Man from the Oval office, the suddenly articulate, that 'loving guy'
        himself,
George W. "As long as you can pay for this war, I'll fight it." Bush.
Anthrax nightmares circled the globe faster than an internet virus.
Doomsday scenarios abounded: Air and water poisoned with
        chemical agents,
Nuclear reactors melting down, governments teetering on the edge.
Collateral Damage is added to the dictionary of double-talk.
While no new words were invented to describe the WTC collapse.
Sex dropped to number seventeen on the Internet hits parade.
Flag sales went through the roof — so much so that flag-makers
        couldn't keep
up with demand, so some Americans did what they do best:
they stole each other's flags.
The Stock Market plunges — so Americans are encouraged to bite
        the bullet
(Get used to it) and buy more stocks.
It's unpatriotic not to go out and shop 'til you drop.
Julia Roberts gives two million dollars to disaster relief.
Telethons raise millions more to help rebuild New York's Financial
        center.
Polls show 90% of Americans support the president, that 98% of
        New Yorkers
Want Mayor Giuliani to stay another term, and 96% think the police
        should
have more latitude in fighting terrorists.

Thus proving that Americans in general, and New Yorkers,
      specifically, have
Very bad memories: is this not the president who was placed in
      power?
Are these not the same cops that have been under investigation for
Over-zealous use/abuse of force? For corruption?
Is not the financial center of the WTC already funded by underpaid
Workers world-wide?
Who did all this?
A man in a cave pulling the purse strings — a man we created,
      in a land we
Created and then ignored, in a region we created (with a little help
      from
our Friends), in a world we created and then 'stepped back from' so
      we could
get back to our arrogant little lives.
Well, this time the revolution will be televised because it's good for
      ratings.

The chickens have come home to roost, baby

— *R.D. Armstrong*

IN THE LAND OF HONEY AND DANGER

Yeah, danger lurks
Danger's the "boogey man"
Our parents warned us about
Right here in this land
Of milk and honey
Or was that supposed to be gold?

Why should the U. S. be immune, huh?
Why? If terrorists can hijack
Those mighty flying machines
And crash into the World Trade Center
And the Pentagon
Why should we feel so safe, secure,
Even those of us with some stocks
And bonds, even those who can while
Away vacations in the Caribbean on
The loveship called "Lollipop?

Maybe that was the goodship,
Yeah, Shirley Temple danced
And sang to it with her golden curls
And now the movies give us
"Pearl Harbor," "Black Hawk Down."
Now patriotism rears itself
In top hat and tails
And it isn't Fred Astaire dancing
On the stairway to the stars either.

Jut think, they, the danger purveyors,
Want Ali to speak out, that the U. S. war
Against terrorism is not about
War against Islam. Heaven forbid.
Perish that notion down a manhole
'Cause danger is not of our own making,
Brother, understand?

Nah, we're not talking anymore
About pulling yourself up
By your bootstraps, that old crap

Gotta live the new lingo
Wearing flags on our lapels
The jingoism dressed in fatigues
Our boys and girls fighting
Over there, in Afghanistan,
For our sanctity of life,
For democracy, that old goat
Who used to point his fingers
At you and off we'd go
Into the wild blue yonder
Killing people who looked like
Some of us in Vietnam,
In Grenada, in Korea, whatever land
Our government warrants
Needs defending 'cause,
Whoa! Democracy's cool,
Just look at Enron scrambling
To save its fat neck
Enron opened up its coffers
And lavished the Republicans
(and the Democrats a bit too)
So the presidency could be
Stolen, could be the throne
It denies itself to be
If there's no royalty in America,
Then what was Camelot about?

Yeah, danger is someone else's
Problem and look what
It's causing us, billions
For war, for security,
For airport screeners to lose
Their low-paid jobs
So immigrants are sacrificed
Every day, so what
If we have to put sky marshals
In the planes now or maybe even
Train passengers to be their own
Defense corps. Heck, all they're doing
Anyway is sleeping or listening

To Eminem or the Backstreet Boys

Danger is packed oh so neatly
In our missiles and smart bombs, danger's even
Disguised in yellow food drops
And it's too bad if the people
In Afghanistan can't tell
The difference between our
Humanitarian aid and the cluster
Bombs that tear limbs and arms apart.

We don't have to watch those disasters
On the big screen anymore.
We've got "friendly fire,"
"Collateral damage" to keep
The patriotism alive.
Somehow, somewhere,
It's got to be an eye for an eye
A bomb for a bomb
A life for a life
Danger can be fun, exciting,
Never forget the honey,
Honey, Though Harry Potter and the
Lord of the Rings can divert us
For a while
And Laura Bush is the big feminist
Now, speaking out about the women
Of Afghanistan, as if women
Here in the U. S. are truly free
'Cause Britney can sway
On Michael Jackson's 30th Anniversary show
'Cause we've got women doctors
and pilots and executives
and equal opportunity women panhandlers

Danger can be a knock on the door
With your friendly FBI just asking
A few questions, especially
If you're Arab or Muslim or Sikh
Or look it, danger can mean

Being locked up like Wen Ho Lee
'cause he's Chinese, accused
of being a spy Danger
can mean your email
And phone line being tapped
We got to do our part, see,
In keeping America safe
So what's a few sacrifices
In the name of security
And democracy?
Dissent? Forget it!
The danger purveyors know
What's best for us

Danger can do the boogie-woogie
Throw you in the air and
You'll land you know not where
Just keep shopping, America,
Even if thousands of workers
Have lost their jobs or in the midst
Of being laid off
We can always make macaroni
And cheese and meat loaf
Tighten our belts
Whether it's Gucci or K-Mart
'Cause this danger business
Is sexy as we ponder whether
to buy that SUV starting at just
$36 thousand, while we watch
On TV the woman who is 50 years plus
But looks older, the newscaster tells us,
As to why she weaves in and out
of traffic holding up
her cardboard sign,
"Need money
Nothing too small
God bless!"

— *Nellie Wong*

ON T. V.

Tuesday was the worst day of my life.
Someone drew a cartoon on the board
Someone who didn't understand that
the terror is real and I cried.
I can't keep it in anymore.
We said we couldn't burn. But we did.
And now I am red with angry flames.
They took the smoke and wrapped it around the city
until everyone was dead. Real dead. Real fear too;
but mostly real people, real people
whose life-strings were torn to pieces.
The red of the fire cursing the buildings
was nothing to the red of our angry, bloody tears.
But the saddest thing isn't the tears that choke the city,
isn't the blood, isn't the smoke and ash,
the saddest thing is that New York's children
aren't young anymore.

Sunday, Dad and I watched T.V.
We saw the orange jumpsuits of the dead firemen
who died that they might restore one thread
in the lop-sided web of life and failed.
He said,

> *It is going to be a big religious war*
> *When I was young it was Vietnam.*
> *Someone should stand up and talk*
> *to say how horrible war is*
> *how terrible hate is*

Well, Dad, this is me.
I'm here.
I'm talking.

— *Mariah Erlick*
   12 years old

LET THERE BE INFINITY

Sept. 11 I was scared shitless
the reggae mom at my kids' school
said they were bombing the world trade center
she said the world was ending
I hurried away from my nervous laugh
as Chicken Little's "the sky is falling, the sky is falling"
tumbled over and over through my frozen thoughts
that kept breaking ice
only to show a fox's hungry face

and then I turned on the tv
and then I trembled
and then I bowed my head
before despair and prayers
uncovered my face to the world

my brother-in-law, the same man
who flew out to hold his first nephew
glowing face to sleeping face
bloodline seeking bloodline
before the newborn blue eyes had faded to brown,
lived in New York

(a New Yorker described seeing
a woman holding her baby who jumped
from one of the burning towers
before he had to look away,
another said he saw a woman holding a man's hand
as they both dropped to their deaths)

— cousins who were cards, phone calls, star trek photos
and the kindness of a movie
        — mailed to our depressed hospitalized son lived in New York

(an Australian man working in the twin towers
described carrying purses and dragging
four exhausted women to safety

down hundreds of stairs,
another survivor with broken legs
spoke on tv of the two unknown women
who carried him to safety)

— a childless aunt slipping sideways into old age
through the decay of independence,
who once sent a gray mouse as big as a mouser
that our little boy dragged through dust and doghair,
she still lived in New York
(an office worker wept as he described
a coworker who refused to leave
a disabled friend in a wheelchair,
who stayed with his friend
until the towers collapsed on them)
these the remnants of my children's Jewish bloodline
offshoots of a family tree
Hitler once tried to chop down
now in danger in New York City

the day ended before we heard they were all alive

over and over I watched the planes hit real life special effects
as the buildings collapsed
and New Yorkers ran from the broiling clouds

my Grandmother once described
grabbing up my father as an infant
and running before black walls
advancing across Kansas prairie,
not knowing if it was dustbowl storms or a tornado,
not knowing whether she would survive this time

these people on my tv, these New Yorkers
were being overtaken
by the first wave of our uncertain future
and in their faces I saw
that they didn't know if we would survive either

when I saw the first newspaper photos
of jumpers with fire at their back,
of trapped people clinging onto a ledge above the clouds,
I wept and sang one of my mother's hymns.

(Oh Lord, my God, when I, in awesome wonder,
my mother's golden soprano
consider all the works thy hand made,
echoing in my mangled version
I see the stars, I hear the mighty thunder,
where the stars are stripped down and thunder
thy power throughout the universe displayed
is manifested over and over on tv
as buildings collapse down around
How great thou art, how great thou art!
all our hopes of safety
Then sings my soul, my Savior God, to thee:
all our hopes of sanity
How great thou art, how great thou art!)

pacing around the apartment
I became another human animal
caged by national circumstance

that night at a UUCB evening service
I couldn't stand up, couldn't speak
because my throat was roughened with unshed tears
with unshed fears
with unspoken names
of relatives,
of unnamable media-portrayed victims,
of future racist victims
who might be from my Muslim past

and from the past
Arabic names roll off my tongue
and the first Sura of the Qur'an/Koran
rises up to protest
terrorist promises

(Bi ism 'allaah ar rah. maan ar rah. iim
In the Name of Allah, Most Gracious, Most Merciful)
— in Mercy and Grace my dead niece and great grandmother were
      so named
(Al h.amd li 'allaah rabb al aalamiin
Praise be to Allah, the Cherisher and Sustainer of the worlds)
— let these spirits, this spirituality, help sustain and cherish those left
      behind on this world
(Ar rah.maan ar rah.iim
 Most Gracious, Most Merciful,)
— **gracious** adj. 2 compassionate **merciful** adj. showing mercy
(Maalik yawm ad diin
Master of the Day of Judgment)
how will the terrorists stand up, how will we stand up on that day?
('Eyaaka na bud wa 'eyaaka nastaiin
Thee do we worship, and Thine aid we seek)
reverence, love, admiration, sustenance, all sought by so many
(Ihdinaa as. Siraat Al mustaqiim
Show us the straight way,)
— but 1.2 million tons of rubble block New York City streets
(S.iraat 'Allaziina an amta alayhim Ghayr al
maghd ub alayhim wa laa ad. D.aalhin
The way of those on whom Thou hast bestowed Thy Grace,
those whose (portion) is not wrath, and who go not astray)
— Grace only bestowed on those who do not go astray
who are not angry, wrathful mobs promising vengeance
(on the tv I see crowds waving unreadable signs and flags in all
      colors
of humans angry and lost in the mob)

I once memorized this Sura
I once upon a time read all of the Qur'an/Koran
I know it never said
to kill the innocent,
nowhere does it say
to create 3,000 ghostly voices
to rise up from a concrete grave

and then Ibrahim's name clutches my heart
over and over, Ibrahim
being beaten, harassed, killed
because he is Arabic
his laughing face that taught me to love him and myself
is Arabic,
his name, Khattab — which means to write,
the name I kept as a guiding star into my future,
his name is Arabic and a marker
just as the Star of David
marked my children's Siegel ancestors
for extermination

fourteen years in love with Ken
married a decade
to an ex-New York ex-Jew hippie
and still I felt the loving burn Ibrahim left on my heart

a name from the Palestinian diaspora
a name from my first dead marriage

I stood on the hill behind UUCB
where the necklace of cities and night
were all that were between me
and wherever Ibrahim was
and I finally said his name
and spoke to him and sang to him

(Burn, Burn or all is lost
Let's stop a second Holocaust)

I thought of his family shot up in Lebanese refugee camps
his mother starving under siege
by Christian Lebanese and Jewish Israelis
and Ibrahim retreating back
into the madness of being the13 yr old who just lost his father
so finally I divorced the 13 yr old
who wanted to go save his mother without me

I thought of the children
my son at ten crying for people he'd never met
a Pakistani friend's son kept home for days
in a tiny apartment filled with the footsteps of fear
-a lawyer who held her sons until they slept
and then wept that they might become soldiers

I was afraid to count the nuclear bombs
we have stockpiled against the truth of our future

I am still counting the days
other people want their Gods to number for us
and I want infinity to become the universal count
just infinity

— *Debra Grace Khattab*

(*UUCB stands for the Unitarian Universalist Church of Berkeley)

NOTES ON OSAMA SPOTTINGS

osama spotted like
victims of rocky mountain
tick fevers

osama spotted like
jaguars ocelots snow leopards
in sites of big game hunters
in the mountains
on the prairies white
with foamingx from
the big house

osama spotted amongst
the homeless in too many
cities favelas refugee camps
in too many places
for these reports to be
believed by journalists with reputations
and credentials to protect

osama spotted replying
to CIA recruitment ads
in the new york times
whose invisible foot notes state
we have turned mandela
over to the south african security branch
we gave them every detail
what he would be wearing
the time of day just
where he would be
they have picked him up
it is one of our greatest coups

osama spotted in old greece
the best of china the sudan
or upper egypt guatemala
Iraq panama

libya managua
grenada hanoi
Havana haiti
islamabad kabul
attica brobdinnag
on old flatbush avenue
a man on a mission
pushing white powders
to some home boys
colombiano death squads
some how missed out on

Osama spotting
Its catching on
all over like
the spanish flu

— *QR Hand*

SMALL SACRIFICES

"Patriotism is the last resort of scoundrels"
Samuel Johnson said. Sorry, this ain't Vietnam
or "Trail of Tears." After 911 fire storm,
I'd enlist in the army if I weren't 62.
Politicians urge shopping to keep America strong,
But stay alert. Some intellectuals advocate
bombing enemies with love, claim evil is relative.
Bullshit. Who speaks for the innocent dead?
I wanna make bullets, car pool, Condemn SUVs
to crushers, tear sheets for bandages, break diplomatic
relations with Saudis, inspect suspicious packages
& junk mail with rubber gloves. Charge Politicians,
CEOs & lobbyists who profit from middle east oil
with treason. Guard a bridge or tunnel with M-16.
Scan Gulf coast & skyline for terrorists
& saboteurs. Ride shotgun on airline, train
or Bus. Patrol Alaska pipeline in armed Humvee.
Most of all, serve on board drafting sons
& daughters of rich & famous standing
on ground zero of freedom in Houston, Chicago,
Atlanta & Hollywood snorting cocaine,
counting stock portfolios, guzzling beer,
getting laid on ecstasy in Enron & Andersen
boardrooms & college dorms as they watch
soot-covered helmeted Iron men retrieving
human remains in Manhattan on CNN until 2004
& soldiers carry flag-draped coffins of fallen brothers
unloaded at Dover—nation's small sacrifice
so Americans can continue life as usual,
go on another shopping spree.

— *Gerald Wheeler*

THE WEAVERS

Afghan refugee
children hunch over looms,
shoulder to shoulder,
in dim rooms
10 hrs a day for food,
their tiny nimble fingers
moving swiftly
up & down threads
of wool, tying knots
of destiny weaving
stars, birds, sun
crescent moons,
& harvest's bounty—
images now shrouded
in hoods with grid-masks,
black smoke
& orange flames
on landscape of dust trails,
rock & stone.
Sometimes
the ground shakes
from explosions,
loud robotic chants
& rocking shadows
of sequestered boys
led by mullahs
in other rooms,
as hunkered robed men
in caves
weave hate,
plotting against freedom
& themselves.

— *Gerald Wheeler*

BURKA WOMEN

Imprisoned behind adobe ruins,
their fingers scarred & swollen
from shelling nuts & beatings
by religious police for sneaking
daughters to secret reading lessons,
scavenging firewood & food,
or playing with kites & balloons.
Their meshed faces grated by fear,
bodies shrouded like ghosts,
they trek bleeding landscape,
stumbling over rock graves
of loved ones murdered by the Taliban.
Taliban led by robed, bearded men
hunkered in caves of shadows
& terror planning evil under sky
streaking tracer fire & contrails
of jet bombers sent by liberators.
The burka women kneel by bomb craters,
hunch over exploded flour sacks,
scoop hope with calloused hands.
They meet strangers like them,
carrying sleeping infants & children,
follow a one-legged man hobbling
on a stick who tried growing wheat
in a mine field. His dark eyes glint
first light of Kabul. He hears a soft voice
whisper, "Soon we'll shed these veils
& hoarded dreams, recognize our sisters
in public, walk to work
& our daughters to school."

— *Gerald Wheeler*

THAT TUESDAY NIGHT

That Tuesday night, after the towers
burned & fell down-
town, after watching them crumble—
unlike the one Paul Newman
saved in—*Towering Inferno*—
from the plaza in front of Rosenthal
Library, after walking home
from the subway in the yellow
summer twilight, gagging
on the acrid air and looking
at the thick sooty column rising
downtown where the towers
had loomed Gargantuan on the skyline
for over three decades,
I went to wash my face,
as though cold water and soap
would wake me from this dream
of violence and violation,
and saw that man in the mirror,
red-rimmed eyes, yes, but
the same sagging sixty-five-
year-old skin, the same thinning,
graying hair above the same lined
forehead, and I knew that he
was lucky to have lived
to sixty-five—too young for WW II
and Korea, too old for Viet Nam—
lucky to have lived his soft
American life without much fear
from abroad, except spotting airplanes
as a kid and catching a breath or two
as JFK stood down the Russians in '62,
and in the glare of the bathroom light,
the sirens screaming just up the street
at St. Vincent's, I knew nothing
could ever make me
safe again.

— *George Held*

ON WORK, LUCK, ROOTS, DEATH
AND OTHER DEBTS

for John Nichols

Don't give up on your blessings,
before they finish.

Life is too short for hate
and other diseases, too long for even one death row,
one cell on death row. One breath.

To go beyond books.
If you want to see in the dark,
turn off the lights.

You have five miracles
at the end of each wrist,
and five miracles
at the end of each ankle,
they need to fly
at least once a day.

It is time to ask the Redwoods
their views on chainsaw control,
it is time to listen to their roots
holding the earth against 25 ton bulldozers,
we could even go down
and register their roots to vote,
if that's not asking too much.
See Julia Butterfly Hill
for the spiritual translation.

For the lives of Animals see Peter Singer,
for the ethics on being a human being,
spend time with Simone Weil
and Dorothy Day.

Are we overrated as being superior
to all species? after all, we do the rating.

The poor of the earth never commit suicide,
they just go on living

their death.

Today is Veterans' Day, 2001,
so I remember you, Colonel
from my three years in the Marine Corps, far
sighted and resourceful,
you were always out there searching
for the perfect cemetery.
At the end of this Veterans' Day,
all I remember and know is Ron Kovic, still
running out there ahead of us.

Why does the Detroit of my youth keep sinking
without hope without drowning?
why does the black male neck
still burn through the rope?

The wealthy elite and the wretched of the earth,
thank you, Frantz Fanon,
have one thread between them,
neither one worries about money.

I can believe in the soul easier than God.
You should not believe in what is easy.

Again, you will end your death penalty of murder,
or sink as a nation. You will bury this last
deformed descendant from the dark ages,
and its black plague of racism,
or sink as a nation.
If you still do not see,
look on it as a kind of toilet training,
like the rest of the civilized world.
See Albert Camus on the guillotine death penalty.
You pay the penalty.

It was complete luck, wasn't it?
How else could I have known
Lake Superior would drain
into the Petaluma River.

A shouting, "Hey! You! Over there in that tree,
sitting up there again stark naked,
what the hell are you doing being alive
after sixty? In my apple tree!"
"Don't shoot! I'm not eating your apples,
I'm still watching
the Milagro Beanfield War!"

I have always trusted teenagers
before adults. The river
before the desert.
Our youth our precious youth,
those who grow up every day watching Lie TV,
will not grow up.

Love your enemy,
it will wreck his reputation ———

Two shadows are falling in Lower Manhattan,
they are falling through the deep Great Lakes
across the nation to the tables in North Beach,
they are falling from one wide crater of ashes,
ashes of steel buried with the ashes of breath,
you can see the two shadows falling all night,
you can see them again falling every morning,
you can trace a finger through the two shadows
on your plate, you can try to wash them down
as they fill your glass, your mirror, your window,
they are falling over us into the smaller plates
of children and the children are tasting them,
the shadows are on their tongues, on their light.
The two shadows move through us to the Pacific,
they are on its beaches, on its tides, on its salt,
the Pacific takes both of them into its shadow.

— *Eugene Ruggles*

DIRGE

There is always some right wing-nut with his hand on the kill button.
There is always some left wing sheep wagging his white tail.
The vast majority just want to get on with life;
have a drink, wink at the pretty possum on the stool across the room.
Me, I want to write poems that dance with the invisible.
Give words to the speechless, shout into the cone of
deafness, you're all a bunch of flaming loonies-
Give comfort to the suffering fools.
Of course its young men and women in uniform wanting to
stand for their flag that makes poetry possible.
Makes dancing flesh. Makes guns for butter
more than a rich tasty dish. Of course we kill anyone
who is honestly nonviolent. Step up to the plate
Mister Martin Luther King Jr. and take your swing at the bullet prize.
Give peace a chance Mr. Lennon your skull a pincushion
of jail-ish laughter. O Gandhi; lets kill him with naked little girls
just to make sure he's still pure as rice.
In fact we kill everyone don't we MS Death, it our only way of life.
Only some of us go jumping life, falling fruit out of
a soulless skyscraper. Or wearing our badges of cloudfull
concrete disappearing with endless bravery.

Some of us call God to come see us in our glory.
God being God backs both sides
on the off chance some war will actually ding a winner.
God never wants to get caught with his pants down
and a good player always hedges his bets.
So let's stop blaming the sky, after all it's only
a theory air exists anyway, a crazy hypothesis,
a schoolboy shouting look at me breathe.
Look at me shoot my finger gun.
A baker with a bun in the oven
eating the flesh of sons and daughters.
A candlestick maker lighting millions of tiny blue souls.
A rub-a-dub peace marcher giving the finger to
a flag wearing freak from some third world war.
Let's all put on our togas and feed some Christians
to the lions, lions are always hungry and circus

games have worked hard for our attention.
Let's all wear turbans and confuse the thought
police with our spiritual donuts.

This isn't a cry for stop. This is a poem
just one killing short of a diatribe.
This is a plea for more. After all war has always
bled, sulked and sung. Let's invent something called fire and man.
No lets steal fire from the Gods. Let's chain each other
to rocks and dine on endless liver. Let's never listen
to women, after all who can hear them through their veils,
mumbling, walking so many paces behind.
We like it this way, the blood on our hands.
We hate it this way, why won't they leave us alone?
Let's rip off the veils, unbind all feet
and follow women's knowledge.
Let's reinvent the wheel in the form a Goddess.
Were just spinning away in our cocoon.
Dancing our sweet fragrance, the bubbles of the hot tub
make us look up, see the star burst butterfly then fade away
disappearing into the soft quilt of black, that's always around us.
Only the sun sears us blind.
Giving a brief sense of shinning.
The star burns itself alive.
The star burns itself dead.
Matter remains,
in the universe unchanged.
Millions of years of getting it right.
Millions of years of getting the light here.
To live in times we get it wrong, such
a lovely curse damned. This is the dance
of what next? The fatal twist.
A cha-cha-cha we can never know the coming
step. Keep moving, I feel a slow dance inching on.
Let's hold each other close and listen to
the music one more time.
That song we keeping singing
those words burrowing into our lips
that buzzing melody of grief
and kiss. Those fat greasy tears.

That dirge we call
life. That spinning jig
to the dying end.
Nothing sound
madness our only
music.

— *Gary Mex Glazner*

THANKSGIVING EVE, 2001

Today
I sort ruin,
lifting shards of concrete and shovels of rubble
picking up a bracelet attached to an arm attached to
nothing
which I carefully - reverently - place in a bag with a label
then pass to Mike
(who has a brother we hope to find)
who marches it to the refrigerated truck
waiting a block away.

Tomorrow
when they make me stay home,
before
I sit with my family
at the long table
heavy with turkey and stuffing and cranberries and mashed potatoes
            and gravy
and
three types of pumpkin pie
where I will pretend to stuff myself while
distantly catching up on the lives of my sister's family
who visits only every other year,
and before
going through the motions of chortling
with my brothers for the thousandth time about
the night we and four of the Stopich boys picked up
Mrs. Delanko's VW Beetle and
set it on her front porch because she wouldn't let
her daughter Amanda
go out with the remaining Stopich boy,
after which
I will retire to the family room to watch football and
eventually nod off
to be later awakened to say goodbyes and
dry dishes and
put kids to bed

then myself
to lay awake until the 5:00 alarm lets me
put on my digging clothes
and go back,

before all that
I'll lead the grace.
I can't imagine where I will begin.

— *F. John Sharp*

SOUTH TOWER, 96TH FLOOR, CORNER OFFICE

Fresh air seduces me.
"Come where you can breathe," she says.
There is no breathing here;
air is poison, searing, near solid.

To live I must lean and breathe.
Soon the flames will touch me,
push me to lean farther.

Past leaning is flying.
Flying is freedom;
freedom is choice.

The hatred behind me
soon will force choosing.
I hope I have the courage
to choose to fly.

— *F. John Sharp*

THE MAGICIAN IN MOURNING

"And much it grieved my heart to think
What man has made of man."
—Wordsworth

The first day of November —
And this morning,
The Magician hid from me —
He stayed behind in the box.
I only discovered him
On returning the rest of the pack
From our daily morning exercise.
He's never done this sort of thing before.
Unlike the Fool
Whose unpredictability
I have come to expect,
The Magician has always been
Dependable, stalwart and true —
My close companion
Ever since he began
To visit me in dreams
Even if he doesn't show his face
On a daily basis,
I always feel his presence.
It's reassuring to know
He's always there
Taking his place
Like the rest of us
In life's random shuffle.
I'm quite concerned about him
This sulky behavior is very uncharacteristic
Especially on the first day of a new month
When he's always on hand
To lead the way forward.
Perhaps he's unwell
Come to think of it,
I haven't seen him —
No, not even once

Since 11 September.
Perhaps that day,
And all that has followed since
Have broken even him.
I can just see him now
Huddled in his little wooden box
Handling listlessly the once so
Proud and promising
Tools of his trade —
The disc of this great bountiful Earth,
The sword of mental clarity,
The wand of creative power,
The cup of human kindness.
Perhaps even he
Can no longer bear to see
How we have defiled
Such gifts

— *Donna Suzanne Kerr*

SACRAMENT

"They lived among us as neighbors."
- *woman interviewed about the September 11 conspirators*

is it jihad? is it crusade? ashes to ashes
dust to dust at the back of my throat
proteins atoms asbestos her snake tattoo his scar and DNA
in the valley of the shadow of death
in the canyon of heroes and there we wept
when we remembered it was nagasaki
is it nagasaki? is it inquisition?
i wonder where memories lodge in ashes
to ashes flame to wax, wax to grime rain-faded flyers
smell of crematoriums the dead are always with us
living among us as neighbors is this rwanda?
wine to blood bread to body
my exhalations stink with her snake tattoo
his scar and DNA taken upon my tongue
extreme sacrament of sacrifice and communion
blessed be the fathers who have sinned
living among us as neighbors
demanding allegiance cultivating silence
because fathers know best because women are unclean
and children unpredictable
because children ask the best questions and no father is safe
is it jihad? is it crusade?
were you there when they crucified my lai
allende? amadou? were you there
taking pride in skin color flag faith
in oklahoma before oh my god it was
one of our neighbors living among us?
each night with myrrh with cypress
and cool eucalyptus i wash my dread
locks of the stench of official sanctimony
the stink of burning plastics and of our neighbors
who loved and lived among us
i try to wash that man right out of my hair

i try to wash that man right out of my hair
i try to wash that man right out of my hair
and send him on his way

— *Eva Yaa Asantewaa*

WTC BOOM BOX:
THE SUBWAY JOKE UNSOUNDED

the room is empty except for the drums
    except for inevitable rhythms
unsounded in the gathering fog
    You are now writing me lost letters
falling through the fog into empty time

 "Fewer people at rush hour in the subway"
I silently joke. You would have appreciated
    that comment: Thousands dead and You among them
in the chemical heat of the transit stairway
    I dare not speak this joke aloud
for those who are lucky have survived
    smiling from the newspaper's special sections
in bandages with rescue stories

"Fewer people in the hospital than cops expected"
I silently joke, turning off the TV news.
    "Thousands dead and You among them
no one here in the easy chair hearing my usual laughter.

the room is empty except for the drums
    except for inevitable rhythms
    unsounded in the gathering fog
You are now writing me lost letters
    falling through the fog into empty time

Above, through the window in the ceiling
    live shadows move against the roof
in the windy moon's day
    shape of the trees in starlight
or a touch like water and ash
    by the tentacles of the dreamless Typhon
night creature, devoid of visions
    and searching for the dreaming flesh
Getting the joke I've thought with a silent laugh
    "Fewer people at rush hour in the subway"

"Thousands dead without overcrowding the clinics"
   "Lines will be shorter at commuter gas pumps."

Tentacles of Typhon almost beautiful
   mistaken for the shadows of the tree
touch with water and ash
   roof window looking upward toward scattered stars
the square of moon's light at my feet
   ripples like a school of eels
with the appetites and laws of war

I wish I could show to You these tentacles of Typhon
but You are not here   You are gone
   the room is empty   except for the drums
subway jokes unsounded in the midnight storm

— *Eugenia Macer-Story*

WHO WERE YOU?

On September 11, a man and a woman jumped from one of the burning towers, holding hands...

Who were you, the two who chose to die together?

Secret lovers,
Claiming each other in the sun
On that brilliant morning, your secret set free?

A man and woman, years married,
Trusting each other
Facing life together
One last time?

Senior V.P. and his 'girl'
teamed up wordlessly
to get the grim job done

Casual acquaintances
Who nodded and smiled in the elevator year after year
Clinging to a familiar sight
As the world went mad?

Strangers, meeting at the window
One thought in your frightened eyes
Reaching out - touching,
As your last human act.

Proud father with his daughter, the new M.B.A.
Stockbroker mother with her trainee son

Whoever you were, did it help?
Did you urge each other forward, or leap with one step?
Did the certainty of fingers around fingers, palm against palm,
            ease that
last moment?

You went first, thousands followed
You died together
They each died alone

Did your love give you comfort?
Was your terror softened?

Would it help if you knew
that our peaceful world
Jumped with you that morning,
Fingers outstretched and grasping
Against the onrushing wind?

Everything I knew to be true
Tumbled with you from those towers

And has not
landed
yet

— *Elizabeth Turner*

ASH TUESDAY

I think I recognize you
trudging across my television screen
dazed, like all the other downtown refugees
bouncing off the terror of not one, but two
planes exploding into skyscrapers

I think it is you, heading for the bridge
beard and brows grayed from where ashes two feet deep
fly about like little dirty snowflakes

It might be your voice they report hearing
calling for help on the cell phone buried
beneath tons of concrete rubble
it might be your body, burning, leaping
hand in hand with another, into the air
a thousand feet up

fists to my eyes, I phone, but can't get through
I email your colleagues, your old girlfriend
but no one knows where you are
or who else might be able to reach you

so, falling back into the safety of the rest of us
I turn to whoever I care about is closest
and say hey, I always meant to tell you: I love you
——only to find that same person turning
to do the same to another and another turning to do
the same to me, don't worry, we say earnestly
with valiant intent, we shall overcome

and I am stirred with the stoutheartedness
of all of us; the goodness of our grand reaching
our veins pierced to donate blood, fingerprints worn
away on our workers staunchly rescuing
rallying, oh beloved masses, oh fine and intent people
oh nation of hands outstretched and offering
hey, I always meant to tell you:
I love you

— *Eileen Malone*

OFF THE AIR

My first love was an AM radio DJ
who played my Journey and Foreigner and Air Supply.
I used to call her on the request line
and joke and try to sound grown up.

I still tune in AM sometimes, way out
in Wyoming, late night Montana, Nevada,
where street lights are scarce
and Country/Western makes more sense.

It seems so much further, this week,
the voices seem more than just years or states away
as they tell me how to be an American,
as they tell me how to be a Christian.

When terrorists attack, see, you must weep
in recitations of the Pledge Of Allegiance
which would overflow a high school drama coach with pride,
you must dub patriotic songs so they sound even more patriotic,

and though you mustn't endorse
a caller's use of nouns such as "towel-head" or "camel jockey,"
but, well, they did bomb us, now, didn't
they.

I am a Christian, I am an American
who welcomes advice as I make up my own mind.
I say prayers,
I sing oh beautiful for spacious skies,

but you tell me how to be me
in the same emphases you insist I try Citrical and Jointritis,
and this great laser-sited golf club,
and read this great new book by this great AM radio host,

scattering me, I'm losing your signal
as I forget if our great nation

is under siege
or just has hemorrhoids and a bad back swing;

what do you think,
you who tell me what to think,
should I listen to you
if you were to tell me the patriotic thing to do

is to fly my airplane
into a skyscraper for Jesus?
Teach me, teach me, is this the American way,
is this, this noise in my ears, the ringing out of freedom?

I can't drive in all this static, I need to pull off
on an unmarked highway, park at the saguaro and scrub,
lay back against my bumper and count the countless stars up above
on this gorgeous night of a blossoming autumn,

this final broadcast of summer.

— *Matthew Mason*

THE DEAD HAVE STOPPED RUNNING

They walk
through the air, now,
above the living, with the living,
pressing on our windows,
resting hands on our doors.
The dead swim
through streets and tunnels,
the dead swim in rivers
the living joke about,
but the dead float
on the swells.
We breathe the dead into our lungs,
brush past them in our hurry
down the grey stairs of the subway.
They rest at our coffee tables,
move their fingers across the kitchen counters.
They sit down on our eyes
as we watch television, they thumb through
our morning papers before we've yet bent
to pick them up, they slip through doors with us
as we zip our jackets and walk to the park
where the dead stand rigid
on tree leaves waving in the wind.
We have ceased our old segregations,
we live with the dead;
these silent neighbors we never noticed before
ride up elevators with us,
surprising us when they exit
on the floor where we live.

— *Matthew Mason*

BECAUSE

because you can't see the bodies—
snails, fish, fungus gnats, rare flowers—
tumbling out of a building,
because trees, rivers, ecosystems
perish quietly, not spectacularly,
because it's not on CNN
with heroics of firemen and policemen,
because it's not right on front of you
like a disaster movie, wrapped up
in a hollywood package
with villains and a harrison ford-like hero,
it's easy to close your eyes
pretend it doesn't exist.
it does.
redwoods, yellowstone, salmon,
arctic national refuge,
everglades, crystal cave—
going, going, gone... to the highest bidder,
our baser nature, the time
between the alarm clock and door lock,
gotta get to work, drink that cup of coffee,
read the paper,
smoke a cigarette.
the business of running the world is someone else's,
not yours (you want to believe).
all around you
bodies—sharks, corals,
tigers—falling from trees,
falling from the sky, turning to stone
then shattering when they hit.
a meadow
a meadow flower.
a mosquito
elk
potto
wallaby
skunk.
a gnat
(older than man),

a whale.
we are not
alone
on this planet.
there is no way
we could ever be
alone.
yet,
30 a day
(by some estimates)
species
are knocked from
their towering
towers,
or jump,
or squashed flat—
crispy,
unrecognizable,
or just parts—
no word
has been invented
yet
to describe what this means.
because you can't see the bodies—
because my words drift off
like clouds in the dry air—
because the impact
explosions
2000 degree fire
the steel melting like taffy
collapse of the whole structure—
is invisible,
you drink your morning coffee,
read your paper,
go to work as always,
work all day,
come home,
and go to sleep.
because.

— *dennis fritzinger*

SIX MONTHS AFTER

This is what it means
to understand history,
Tolstoy: We never go
far enough, just credit
the latest Napoleon
with the damage.

Walter Benjamin:
one single catastrophe
which keeps piling up
wreckage...the pile
of debris growing
skyward.

"We all see a piece
of history," said Tony
the fireman, no longer
a boy on probation.
—"It was raining bodies,"
said another, holding
an axe, "I found
a foot encased
in the rubble."

This man with an axe
and a helmet rubbed tears
from his eyes, and that
is what it means
to understand history,
although there is also
the scream and the shriek,
the drumbeat of bodies

striking the roof.
Some say the debris
also speaks.

— *David Ray*

THE DILEMMA

It is once again time to think of what we wish
to say—in stone or steel, aluminum, titanium—

for we can once again prove how high we can
be lifted into the sky and manage to work there,

almost as if on terra firma. But who in that case
will not look out and, like a survivor of a shark

attack, scan the blue for another? And what do
we wish to convey in our message, be it in stone,

be it in metal? Nobody knows, Robert Hughes
wrote, how many drinkers were converted

to Seagram's' whiskey by design of its building,
but we know an edifice is also an advertisement,

as Gio Ponti remarked of the Pirelli headquarters
in Milan. The Parthenon, it could be said,

was an advertisement for the glory that was Greece,
and one can see in what Hitler and Mussolini

ordered built the banality and sterility of Nazi evil,
cast in stone. A building can proclaim the worship

of Mars or Mammon. With twin towers that were
bank and Bourse and beehive of commerce rolled

into one, the World Trade Center aroused love,
but also rage and envy. We were judged as flaunting

our wealth and prosperity; a false impression,
perhaps, but do we want to risk that distortion

of intentions again? Do we wish to provide

once again more lambs for the sacrifice? It cannot

happen again was always a fool's motto
Now we could, if we would, pause for reflection,

a second thought before we prove again how high
we can loft our dreams or how many millions

of rivets we can pop into steel and titanium.
If we are out to advertise, then let us think long

and hard of what our product is to be, and let it
not be simply what the highest bidder bids.

I suggest something on the theme of a peaceable
kingdom, with every nation included in the scene,

and grief and love of earth and all its creatures
emphasized, and with our humility enshrined

as a virtue long lost but at last found and exalted.
That would be a monument, I think, that might

win not rage and envy but solemn meditation.
And let song rise often from this site.

— *David Ray*

BLACK DAHLIA

THE CUPS WE DRINK FROM ARE THE SKULLS OF
ARABS
AND THIS SILK IS THE SKIN OF BABIES.
THE FROTHING ON OUR CHINS
IS NOT RABIES NOR ARE OUR FINGERNAILS
GOLDEN SCARABS.
WE'RE *NORMAL* HUMAN ANIMALS
AND WE ITCH LIKE SCABIES
FOR THE RAPE OF THINGS.
It is ordinary and beautiful
to have the duty
to twist and tease
the lovely glimmering light
we see in things.

Then one day we look about
and hope to put it back
inside,
where once was fresh foam or moss.

But we've made a cross
of wings of birds and butterflies
and it cannot lift off the ground
or push into the soil.
—Where there was a perfume smell
of mulch
now there's the stink of oil
turned inside out,
and finger prints of brightness
gone away.

What
will
we
say
to

all
the
singing
realms
that
try
to
rise
inside
of
us
?

(grahhr)

— *Michael McClure*

A LITTLE RAMSHACKLE SHACK

1

A little ramshackle shack on a hill
blown apart by the wind
door roof and walls lofted aloft and sent flying
no weightier than paper upon which is casually written
a name
twists in the air almost signals goodbye then
suddenly is gone only
bare hillside left behind
a goat now stands upon
two goats a small herd after the wind's died down
straggle along distractedly
chewing

Madame X is led out to the guillotine where a
head once encircled by ermine on a tall neck once
encircled by strings of pearls and glittering diamonds
rolls like a dark pearl into a basket its
eyes rolled heavenward its body relaxed
backward like a flung necklace onto a
marble tabletop in an
empty room after the
ball is over

2

Imagine the precise and daunting gears and
levers of the decree that led to all those innocent
people meeting death at the World Trade Center in
New York September 11, 2001
all the little accumulating gestures and maneuvers that
put them at their desks on schedule in time to die
the horrific fireball of the angel of death who may have
appeared to them all at the last as
cool refreshing waterfalls of light or open
delightful corridors leading to emerald green

gardens so bright with joy they forgot completely
how they got there

we all wonder how we'll die
hoping for a soft bed in a warmly lit room surrounded by
loved ones after a short and not too uncomfortable
illness a kind of light cough or a
stitch in the side and that's all
never imagining falling to the ground from 110 stories in the air
or twisted in molten steel like a tyrant's cage
in suffocating smoke

unthinkable

the high school diplomas the happy
vacation moments in Cancun across a turquoise pool
the epiphanies while reading Moby Dick
the birthday banquets with long-lost relatives
the recent wedding or long-awaited love letter received

it's a lone figure in a woolen hat on a sheer white hillside
whose coat trails the ground and whose
footprints evaporate once the meeting's taken place
it's unfathomable and beyond any human
words devised to describe it
and for all those souls lost in the New York disaster
whose accidental but destined martyrdom is absolutely assured
(except ironically to the fanatically deluded
hell-bound perpetrators of the unthinkable
disaster itself)

there are coats of eiderdown so soft and pearls so ethereally gorgeous
so filled with subatomic music that pours out of
every gap in their weave to envelop the air in
ecstatic choir
and the divine shadow of Truth moves aside to let pour
a radiance so pure every moment set in motion in time
one step after another year after year that led to their
being there in the right place at the

supreme right time
suddenly becomes a series of perfect stepping stones like floating
lilypads over deep black water to a Paradise even our
most ornate imaginations cannot adequately imagine

3

People are very involved with having
faces and eyes and thoughts of their own and
smells in the odorous parts of their
bodies where the human anatomy dictates
they move with a certain self-consciousness which is sometimes
nonchalant and at other times unnatural
they can feel their spines hunched or vertically straight
and how their rib-cages make room for their breathing
people are curious capsules of atmospheres and internal weathers
and at complete ease are either blessed with expansive
horizons or cursed with tics and foibles that
intensely constrain them
a consciousness that may include the Serengeti for example with
all its wild flora and fauna or the
bleached out and tattered prospect of simply
four walls a ceiling and a floor
young ones often betray a jumpy and eager quality
old ones a sleepy and generally exhausted quality though they
may achieve beneficence from time to time as their
bones creak and their nerves ache

but each one is categorically a cosmos and has vivid
cosmological thinking and a deep appreciation of its consequences
and each one experiences the end of the
world when death appears like a
yawning sea to drown them in its
perpetuity

drawing back within it the
essence of their beauty

4

This is the music space
where music is most difficult
this place of joy and horror
sound of fuselage entering steel as if

slicing through butter

this is the silence out of which
all the thrilling chords emerge

this is the space of the silence of souls
at their moment of release

this is the air over a dewy wheatfield
crackling like cellophane in the morning light

this is the music space
voices in a room of those
visible and those who are invisible

I think the music of the spheres
can be heard in this space

it's the sound of life
which takes place without echo
or is nothing but echo

and the original sound is the
sound of God alone audible to Himself
and we are the humming elements of that sound

this is the music space
we hear it this very moment

it's the sound of hooves
and nothing at all like the sound of hooves

it's the endlessly heaving ocean-sound
which turns out to be our blood beating
and the deep tidal push of our own heartbeats

each whisper of love and fear and grief
rises in this music space

and one single note is enough to fill it

and silence itself is part of it

and the silence or the sound that follows it
is also part of it

— *Daniel Abdal-Hayy Moore*

THERE IS SILENCE

there is silence
and there is silent noise
that roars in the head
take up arms of words
events are moving
but when haven't they been?
history is not static, not linear
like they would have you believe
history goes in circles
cycles of rhythms, of signs, of change
listen to the holy molly ghosts
hear their cries, tell you about the utter lies
if we fail to learn from the past
then it will loop endlessly
nothing happens in a vacuum, folks!
stunned silence is for the masses
poets must use their voice
or they ARE silenced!
It's your choice!!!
psychic numbing
is the enemy
anger, fear
are gut reactions
and also danger signals
but for the poets of this torn world
the poem must go on, now is an opportunity
to find the words in the bottom of your soul
do not bury your feelings under confusion
warriors, are trained for battle, but how
do you fight the terror from within?
do you learn to stand in their shoes?
NOTHING HAPPENS IN A VACUUM!!!
PEARL HARBOR, they cry!!! funny but
wasn't that just a Hollowwood movie
huge cornball blockbuster!! Funny that
coincidence?...nothing is a coincidence in this
world people, karma speeds up, and so does the

language, its there to teach us the truth
the truth behind the gloss and gloss over
awake! to the clash of events, hear them sing
in your veins, let the words bleed from the
mirror to the day of unfunny!!!
use the horrible images to create
poetry is not a shallow activity
it takes nerve, and verve, it takes vision
open your eyes, look within, then look without
again, what do you see?...smoke, debris, ideas
blowin in the wind of strange days...
death on the screen, going by endlessly...
remember thousands die of hunger daily
is that less terrible, remember the rain forests
remember the oceans are dying, crying tears are drying
don't be shattered like the black windows of illusion
the moon is still in the sky behind the cruel plumes
pick up a pen, find a place inside that is struck numb
and awaken it with questions, and test the limits....
and go beyond....awaken the pain in the world, sing
through it, to the sun beyond the angry hellish plumes

— *Craig Moore*

GROUND ZERO

What's after or before
seems a dull locus now
as if there ever could be more

or less of what there is,
a life lived just because
it is a life if nothing more.

The street goes by the door
just like it did before.
Years after I am dead,

there will be someone here instead
perhaps to open it,
look out to see what's there —

even if nothing is,
or ever was,
or somehow all got lost.

Persist, go on, believe.
Dreams may be all we have,
whatever one believes

of worlds wherever they are —
with people waiting there
will know us when we come

when all the strife is over,
all the sad battles lost or won,
all turned to dust.

— *Robert Creeley*

ON THE DESTRUCTION OF THE
WORLD TRADE CENTER
SEPTEMBER 2001

I am an American, eyes drooping heavily
at half-mast for the dead and missing of NYC.
My arm outstretched, a pipeline of blood,
a piece of myself to send to the yet living
in the hospitals of Manhattan.

I am Japanese, wearing the white robes
of mourning for the citizens of Nagasaki,
transfixed by the silhouette of a body
on the sidewalk, no dust remaining.

I am German and Jewish and I am
shoveling the ashes from the ovens,
weakening and wondering when my turn will come.

I am Palestinian, my motherly eyes searching
for my wayward boy, there by the fence in Gaza,
a rock still clutched in his hand.

I am a Hutu farmhand whose children played
with the Tutsi neighbors, their throats now slit
and their beds growing cold.

I am a peasant of Sarajevo, a reporter in Chile,
a nun in El Salvador, a monk in Tibet,
a starving child in the Sudan.

I am human, I wrap myself in many colored
flags and shrouds and wail to the heavens
for peace.

I am an American and on this day,
with heavy eyes and arm outstretched,
I am afraid for we are going to war.

— *Cathy Barber*

ONE DAY LAST WEEK

The end of the world
   rained from the sky
      down the breaking floors.

The world turned black and silent.
   In the thick advancing cloud,
      muted screams of the trapped.

Of course it wasn't the end –
   not for us – that will come
      in advancing ice, or some wild

cadmium ganglia of explosion –
   one microsecond of blind light
      before we melt into each other.

But this was more than enough for now –
   people tumbled together,
      chefs and bankers, immigrants

and newly bronzed youth,
   like Icarus, fell out of the sky, silently
      spinning down the chutes of glass,

and over and over again –
   the plane full of still-living people
      beaconed on the tower

full of still-living people,
   the snuff of a moment
      a bright steel and glass candle

melting in on itself.
   You cannot look away,
      each time it's as the first time.

Stories drift loose, first the misguided who turned
    like sheep back to their desks; later
        the personal stories from friends:

the neighbor's son made of plaster and dust
    who crawled free and started walking,
        walking uptown, one foot, then the other

until he could move no further.
    Sitting on the library steps near a lion
        he turned to stone

and out of the gathering smoke
    walked his brother. How
        do these things happen – the odds of it,

the very need of it, and sat beside him
    and held his hand and they cried
        for what had been taken away.

Slowly, eventually, the trains
    pulled out of Grand Central, the ferry
        began to run again to Staten Island,

but oh, all the cars at all the stations,
    empty, unclaimed
and at the airports.

— *CB Follette*

HOME

(before 9/11)

Twenty three years later and I'm walking down twenty eighth and
          eighth in New York City
playing tourist, looking up, head swiveling from side to side
gawking at skyscrapers so anyone would think I hadn't been born
          there,

grown up there, spent my teenage years in Greenwich Village cafes or
in the galleries of museums before I left, before I moved on and
          began to forget
what was beautiful about growing up in New York City's Spanish
          Harlem, how even

the dirty sidewalks above 96th Street glistened after it rained and how
          thunder and lightning
came down in sheets in the summer time and did nothing to assuage
          the humidity
and how when I was fifteen I took girls on cheap dates

by riding the Staten Island ferry back and forth, back and forth,
timing it so that the sun was always setting
on our last trip back to the Battery

so I could bend over to kiss the girl I was with
while the last of the sun's rays turned the oily waters orange
and I could forget about whatever happened yesterday and not have
          to think about

what might happen tomorrow before I rode the subway back uptown
careful never to look anyone in the eye.
The years passed, first in Boston and then in Seattle:

lovers and more lovers, and then the deaths of lovers, and then more
          lovers
followed by marriage and by children, by the purchase of a house
and then one day when I looked in the mirror, I saw

the slender young man, my inseparable companion, gone
and the face in the mirror was different
and knew it was time to go home.

(after 9/11)

If I had come afterwards, would I have been a stranger
limping down the City's dusty streets at high noon,
haze hiding the sun's power and would I have heard the machinery's

mechanical roaring, and the howls and the groans, the wailing and
        the gnashing
of I-beams about to fall and would I have heard fires roaring,
the refusal of flesh to die and of concrete refusing to crumble?

If I had come afterwards, would I have felt like a lost son coming
        home?
Would someone have killed a sheep or fatted a calf to put on a spit to
        cook,
rabbis dancing in the streets arm in arm with junkies, the whores of
        42nd street

scrubbed clean, their faces shining, their lips no longer bruised, their
        breasts full and pendant,
unmarked by hard use? I came home before it happened and stood
        on the stern
of the boat going to the Statue of Liberty and looked up at those
        towers

whose height could not contain
my love for my city and when I turned away, going west again,
no longer the young man I'd been,

I remembered how the light reflected from the harbor
bounced against their windows, remembered tugboats' whistles
        blowing
and how the water spouting from fire boats rose and rose.

— *Carlos Martinez*

KABUL 2002   (FROM DISLOCATIONS)

Kabul seizes your eyes your throat
Hangs heavy in the air
The mountains a vague background suggestion
Los Angeles on a bad day
Minus Venice Beach and Santa Monica

Kabul invades your nostrils
Heat dust petrol daysold oil
Sides of meat in the market buzzing with flies
The runoff dries and cakes in the gutters
Kabul smells of Peshawar

Kabul wakes you at 4am
The discordant stridency of busy dawn cars
Frenetically bound around a roundabout
The policeman parasol-protected
Against the sun heat dust no rain to speak of
Blows his whistle on occasion
As the cars buzzbuzzbuzz like flies

Kabul greets you with destruction
Plane carcasses lined up along the runway
Ghosts of military welcomes past
Bombed out hangars house bombed out planes
Office buildings conduct business as usual
Next to gaping holes in their façades

Kabul marks its memories
In the middle of the main bazaar
An embarrassed and cloaked-in central square
A former Taliban place of execution
We photograph the landmarks
"The Taliban soldiers were here" CLICK
"The United Front shot from here" CLICK
In between, a street full of saplings
Newly cut timber for rebuilding

Kabul teaches its children
In half remaining rooms
Tarpaulins make up the difference
UN protection from the June sun
Classroom posters show the alphabet numbers landmines
The basics of Afghan literacy
The girls proudly recite their lesson
"The value of sharing water"
And jostle to smile for our cameras
The teachers invite us for tea
Later under their burqas
Screens muffling their voices their eyes
I remember their smiles

Kabul drinks tea
Delicate with cardamon
And the warmth of gentle hospitality
Incongruous and optimistic
Like the women and girls smiles
In this bleak and savage place

Kabul goes about its business
Salwar kameez driving donkeys
And burqas towing children
One day things will be better
In the meantime we have to eat

Parwan

Shamari stretches in the sun
The highway a red-dotted line to the Kush
Red for landmines
Remnants of villages, ghost towns elsewhere,
Less romantic here, they are Ruins Remains Rubble

The tanks are everywhere
Lined up along the highway
Like the planes along the runway

But the planes were orderly
Corpses laid out after battle
The tanks are everywhichway
Caught in suspended animation

But Afghanistan Is Rebuilding
Spanking new petrol stations
Smile at passing cars vans trucks
Prettily painted, almost ready for customers
Gleaming new mosques
Dazzling in the midday heat
Prettily painted always ready for customers
Transport and religion
Priorities for national reconstruction

The women teach the value of sharing water
And the children memorize written words
No books to write in or pencils to write with
Water and words are precious things
To be savored relished devoured
But only in moderation
While the men guzzle petrol and prayer

Water and words are precious
The children collect words like jewels
Their mothers stumble over the letters
And dream of becoming seamstresses

Panjshir

The road turns to rubble
And the mountains become visible
The rapids rush brown over rock
Heady excitement of left alone wildness

Climbing high rounding rock water rock
A tank perched impossibly on an outcrop
Like some alien spaceship

Abandoned to an earthly fate

Abandon abandoned abandonment
Words to characterize a country

The Panjshir villages huddle in the valleys
They have managed to stay in hiding
Put their heads down until the battlefire passed
One survives how one can

I saw Massoud's house
Opulence and running water
Next to the running river
I saw Massoud's grave
A killer killed becomes a martyr
A Protector of the People
I shudder in the summer afternoon

Driving home after nightfall
An injured tank points its gun
Directly into our headlights
Sudden and frightening in the Panjshir moonscape

Peshawar 2002

It takes time to cross University Road
No such thing as a break in the traffic
Men lean out leering from buses
Rickshaws and taxis slow enquiringly
Their drivers incredulous to be waved away
A lone western woman crossing the road
Is not a concept here
Westerners ride in taxis rickshaws 4wheeldrives
And women do not venture alone
Through the streets of Peshawar
Peshawar is not a safe place

In pairs trios with children
The women are never alone
But always isolated
Covered heads faces bodies
The women are never invisible
But always anonymous
Threading through the marketplace
The women are never still
But always constrained
Bonded jailed burqaed
Bosses police landlords husbands children
Everyone stakes a claim gets a cut
Peshawar is not a gentle place

In the backstreets of University Town
The traffic thins people disappear
Into the grounds of whitewalled residences
As pristine as Pakistan gets
The trees gardens 4wheeldrives
Clumps of beggars at gateways
Universal giveaways of a city's rarefied space
Where bourgeoisie meets NGOs and UN
Peshawar's protected places

Those who live and work here are nervous
On Friday a carbomb in Karachi
Pedestrians unlucky enough
To be near something American
Already on Thursday a danger warning
Stay within University Town
Unless Absolutely Necessary
I do not stay in University Town
In the dusty late afternoon
The city stirs from hot stupor
Traffic thick again on University Road
Sudden alertness of shopkeepers
As the bazaar bustles and jostles
University Town at a nearby distance
Draws its walls closer around

Peshawar is unsafe

Accompanied by radio antennae and guns
The UN and I climb the frontier mountains
"Welcome to the Khyber pass"
Tourists greeted by signs and soldiers
Welcome to wildness and romantic imaginings
Beautiful breathtaking spectacular magnificent
Words accurate and inadequate
For this seductive and intimidating place
The road winds ribbons round the rock face
No tanks here, just 4wheeldrives and guns
And bustruckloads of those returning
The War Is Over Now
Two hours and fifty-four kilometres
A journey to the edge of lives
Peshawar is a long way away

Shalman sits like a surprise in the valley
A sudden peopling amidst barrenness
A clearing in the mountains
A flat place to pitch tents
Twenty thousand people in a holiday camp
Latrine enclosures like green marshmallows
And shalegrey gravestones like menhirs
Punctuate the beige monotony
Where water and hope are rare
Where Kabul Kunduz Mazar are memories
And Peshawar only a thought

Shalman's fortunes are those of war
Open in January overflowing in March
In April the men line up
There are eight nine ten in our family
One tent is not enough
In May the womenchildren line up
For medicines and extra flour
In June the families pack up
We can go back now

The War Is Over
Memories picked up where left off
But Kabul Kunduz Mazar are not the same
Do not have buildings jobs homes
Do not have food do not have water
And only the women have tents
Blue like the screened-off sky
The returnees return again across mountains
Peshawar is a gentler and safer place

— *Dr. Bronwyn Winter*

SKYSCRAPER APOCALYPSE

Two months before the terrorist attack
a 16-year-old walked into a hospital
in New York City
handed the receptionist a note—
"Please donate my organs in case of death"
then blew his brains out in front of her.
Six hours later his removed eyes
were transplanted into empty eye-sockets
of a 60-year-old woman
blind since birth
who two months later
turns on morning TV to see
skyscraper apocalypse.

A week before the terrorist attack
a woman stopped her car
on a bridge in Seattle
during morning rush hour traffic,
got out, climbed over the railing,
stood on the ledge looking down.
Commuters caught in the traffic jam
fearing they'd be late for work
started yelling "Jump! Jump!"
even started making a banner
encouraging her to jump
till she finally did.

The terrorist at the controls
and his fellow terrorists
in the cockpit
had big grins as the jet
slammed
into the skyscraper
believing they were instantly transported
to an endless orgasm
in a paradise of beautiful girls
because their suicide terrorism

was a heroic martyrdom
that made God happy.

No one ever saw two
of the tallest buildings
on Planet Earth
burn and collapse
in less time than it took
the *Titanic* to sink.
Till now.

Flashback to Walt Whitman 150 years ago
standing where the World Trade Center Towers
would stand
looking up at circling seagulls
looking down at him
little knowing
skyscrapers so high
would be built
or jet planes exist
hijacked
by deranged fanatics
deliberately crashing
into those skyscrapers
murdering thousands
because they think
God wants them to....

How the jet appeared to be
swallowed by the Tower
entering it like a hangar
and a split second existed
before
the explosion—
just enough time
for office-workers sipping coffee
reading their newspapers
to drop through the demolished floor
and through the torn-off roof of the jet

to suddenly be side-by-side
with airplane passengers
gaping each other in horror
as the fireball engulfed them....

Flashback to victory parade
in downtown Manhattan
after Persian Gulf War—
snowstorms of confetti
wafting down on drunk celebrators
from triumphant skyscrapers above,
from soaring and mighty skyscrapers above.

How does it feel to be exploded into human flesh confetti?
How does it feel to be decapitated, dismembered, disemboweled?
Some were burned beyond recognition. Some were burned to ash.
Some were vaporized. Some were squashed or crushed
into shapes never forgotten
by those who discover
or even imagine them.

Makes me wish Immortality exists
for the victims and their loved ones,
even if it doesn't exist,
makes me wish it true for them.
Makes me wish there were a heaven
that could compensate for this hell.

One American said
he wouldn't be satisfied
till he saw children in Afghanistan
running down the street on fire screaming.

Another said he wouldn't feel right
till he could be in Afghanistan
and throw a grenade
into a schoolbus full of children.

Another said he told his girlfriend as she ate dinner

there are more rats in New York City than people
and couldn't get out of his mind the image the thought
of thousands of rats descending into the site at night
following dark shadows under debris,
under twisted metal girders, down, down
to eat body parts of mothers, fathers,
brothers, sisters, lovers, friends....
she said she wished he hadn't brought it up
while she was eating.

Rats don't know about hijackers or what caused
the magnificent Towers to come crashing down,
but it makes them happy night after night
a midnight feast under
subterranean skyscraper rubble.

If only the terrorists had been more into
tightrope-walking between the Towers
to the delight of cheering onlookers
to draw media attention to their cause
and debate it in pastoral settings
with fountains and jugs of wine.
If only the terrorists had gone to costume parties
dressed up as their favorite skyscrapers,
got drunk, lit each other's skyscraper on fire
and laughing jumped in the swimmingpool.
If only they had believed cutting snowflake designs
from folded paper during a blizzard
and unfolding them in front of each other
pleases God more than explosions of body parts.
If only the terrorists had been more into
watching butterflies emerge from their chrysalises
or dragonflies emerge from their nymphs.
If only the terrorists had been more into pterodactyls,
believing the more life-size models of pterodactyls
the more we are in awe of Allah's handiwork.
If only the terrorists had spent their lives trying to prove
the world annihilates itself and reappears just as it was
a million times a second.

If only the terrorists had embraced as their mission
to evangelize to every nation and religion
there are enough advanced civilizations in the Universe
for a trillion different utopias
from a trillion different planets
from a trillion different galaxies
to pay Earth a visit every nanosecond.
If only the terrorists had been more into wandering
snowy midnight winter neighborhoods
looking for snow angels children made
to lie down in them and ask their blessing.
If only the terrorists had been more into deer
eating from their outheld hands.

Have the winds blown enough
that by now all of us have breathed
particles of the burned-up corpses?
Sooner or later all of us will inhale
invisible remains of the incinerated victims,
their atoms and molecules spinning in space
transported by breezes little-by-little
dispersing outward spreading outward
till all of us have inside us through breathing
the vanished corpses that will never be found
but that found us and became
buried within us....

Meanwhile a seagull circles and soars
where the skyscrapers once stood
looking down at the human ants below
wondering what happened
to the two huge monoliths
and the shadows
they cast on each other.

Meanwhile four miles from ground zero
in the Frick Gallery near Central Park
in a room next to the marble courtyard
with its pillar'd colonnade and arching skylight

with its fountain pool with two gold frogs at either end
spurting continuous long arcs of water—
St. Francis in Ecstasy by Giovanni Bellini,
painted the same year Columbus set sail
in search of a New World,
still shows St. Francis barefoot in his monk's robe
emerging from his hermit cave
leaving behind his desk with closed Bible and human skull
looking up with arms outstretched in awe
to fields and woods and mountains
as the sunrise engulfs the world
in the light of another day.

— *Antler*

HOW DO I EXPLAIN THE HORROR?

How do I explain the horror the madness
the chaos?
How do I begin to make sense of it for
myself? to understand. how do I explain it
to my four small children?
How do I make them feel safe? how do I
protect them?
How do I explain atrocities? how do I
explain the number six million Jews killed
by the nazi's in concentration camps?
and what about the five million ethnic
minorities
killed in those same camps by the nazi's?
The five million that history has
forgotten to grieve for.
What flame burns for the gypsies for the
Catholics for the gays? their deaths never
mentioned forgotten
We do not even shed a tear expel a breath
for them
Their spirits are lost to us
floating in terror, trapped in screams in
agony in torture
How do I explain the twin towers of New
York to my children?
The 3000 lives lost
How do I reassemble a life for them now
after that?
Do I cradle them in my arms wrap them in
barbed wire
shelter them in electrified fences
surround them on an island of concertina
wire whose razor edges will not protect
them my children or shelter their spirits
from the barbs of hate intolerance and
injustice?
How will they move in the narrow spaces

America is constructing?
Tightly quietly carefully prayerfully
moving in amerika
So I pray and keep moving, my lungs fill
with air
I revel in the beauty of morning in the
rocks that shimmer
in the late afternoon sun
and I laugh again and
often as I watch my dogs
and their kind loving faces
I embrace my family my children my
students my friends my spirit I want to
wrap them in prayers to protect them
In a blanket of sacred smoke clothe them
in prayer ties
cover them in protective tobacco, cedar
and sweet grass
and send prayers to all the children
praying and dying in Afghanistan and
Palestine surround them in song, shield
them in drum songs enveloped in your
prayers.

— *diego davalos*

A FRONT ROW SEAT IN HEAVEN

The world Trade Center buried
in rubble
Bands of Palestinians celebrating
in the street
King Kong's balls cut off
but erection still firm
Poets flooding internet pages
with wounded words
dressed in dark shrouds
Death in the name of Christ
Death in the name of Allah
from the inquisition to the
not so holy wars
from the Salem witch trials
to New York City

Dial a prayer
Promise a terrorist
a front row seat in heaven
Jews, Arabs, Catholics
and Protestants guided
by God's pointed finger

America's heart severed
Onward Christian Soldiers
marching to war
Day of death
Day of rich women walking
poodle dogs
Day of stockbrokers crying
Day of the innocent dying

Flags unfurling
Old Glory about to be prostituted
by pimp politicians
and unindicted corporate criminals
No eulogy for New York City

No eulogy for Bin Laden
No eulogy for Israel
No eulogy for suicide bombers

Capitalism shaped like a coffin
floating across TV screens
New York City bathed in blood
and screams
New World Order stuffed
in a casket
Blame the immigrants
Blame the Arabs
Blame the Jews
Blame the Christians
Blame the Holy Ghost
lying mortally wounded
on the East Coast
When the truth is that
people are not good
to each other
people are not good
to each other,
and suicide comes easy
when your lot in life
is such that you
have nothing to lose
and are promised
a front row seat
in heaven

— *A.D. Winans*

THE BELL TOLLS AGAIN

And if we don't act violently now we will see this go on and on and on.
—Lawrence Eagleburger, former United States Secretary of State

At the World Trade Center
The doormen working minimum wage
Died with the stockbrokers
Making a million dollars an hour
They all died together
Just as they were born
Dust unto dust
Militant arrogant American dust
Humble kind destitute dust
Of the wretched of the earth
They all died together
Because human flesh keeps aspiring higher
And keeps hating its own aspirations
Because no one has yet truly learned
Forgiveness
What a lesson to learn—
What a hard way to learn it!
What did we do to deserve
Such terrible teachers?
We forgot that they were
Human too
And they failed to realize
There were other ways to teach it
Though perhaps none
Quite so effective—
"And they call us
the human race!"
said a wise man long ago
who had not learned the lesson either
and who was also
blown away.

— *Gerald Nicosia*

PEACE   INVOCATION AFTER 9/11/2002
INVOCACION A LA PAZ -
9 DE SEPTIEMBRE/ 2002.

PEACE did you shudder
when two airplanes
like cold knives
cut through the two
highest towers of New York?
and anger lifting its hot face
untied the sleeping
giant of WAR?

PAZ te estremeciste
cuando dos aviones
cual frios cuchillos
atravesaron de un corte
las mas altas torres
de Nueva York?
y caliente el rencor
desato
el gigante dormido
de la GUERRA?

PEACE did you shake
at the collapse
of the Twin Towers
and the Pentagon?
— power world icons
of money and war.
Horror inflicted
upon us a mortal wound
as our beloved
catapulted down
to definite emptiness.

PAZ te conmovio el colapso
de Las Torres Gemelas
y del Pentagono

simbolos mundiales
del poder
de la guerra y del dinero.
El Horror nos penetro
con una herida mortal
mientras los que amabamos
caian al precipicio del
vacio definitivo.

PEACE I Invoke
your dear name
in hope,
i invite you
to be born with me.
Clean your nascent
moonlike face.
Earth is contaminated
with hatred
and inconsolable pain.

PAZ invoco tu nombre
querido,
con esperanza.
Te invito a nacer conmigo.
Limpia tu carita
de luna recien nacida.
La Tierra esta contaminada
con el odio
y el dolor inconsolable.

PEACE teach us to speak
a common language
to include the voiceless
and the silenced of our planet.
Hold reconciliation,
mediation
in the warmest embrace.
Deliver justice
with full hands

to the Earth's children.
Remove from the roots
the visceral
impoverishment
of the spirit.

Paz ensenanos
a hablar
con un lenguaje
en comun
que incluya
a los que no
pueden hablar
y a los que
silenciaron para siempre.
Abraza
con tu calidez
a la reconciliacion
y a la mediacion.
Distribuye la justicia
a manos llenas
entre los hijos
de la Tierra.
Arranca de raiz
el empobrecimiento
viceral del espiritu.

PEACE I invoke
your name in hope.
Brush away our
continuous nightmare.
Extend your bridal veil
over our humanity,
and join us to learn
to love our differences.

PAZ Invoco tu nombre
en esperanza.
Borra nuestra continua

pesadilla.
Extiende tu velo de novia
sobre nuestra humanidad
y unenos para aprender
a amar nuestras diferencias

— *Teresa G. Lee*

ON THE FALL OF THE WORLD TRADE TOWERS

I
When hate crimes last in a bombscare loomed
Then and only, a skinny boy
Slipped on fresh graves for the newly doomed
Stretchered in shock, we didn't know why.

Where were the gone when the World Trade fell?
Down went black in a slam of smoke
Heart broke twice when a single arm
Lay in the rubble
Swollen and still.

I'm staying in. I saw the exploded sky
through memory's wind crushed window. It's so hot
It burns you when you think of it and cry.

I just gave birth to twins as cold tomorrow
creeps in Shakespearean pace to Life Insurance.
Out Heaven's window, fail safe, safe fail
Life on the dole, (black hole, black hole.)

Love's teeny ashes crackling in a heap
and night sweeps bitter through the firetruck mist.
Where are the ones they died to save?
Seat of the soul, (black hole, black hole.)

When if ever, the firemen died
Brave as babies who touch the stove
innocent still but now afraid,
bury the merry — arrive alive
Out Hell's window, set sail, set sail)
roll of the dice, (black hole, black hole.)

Hijackers gone, we are one lame country
What was the cause they tried to save?
the sky is falling — black choppers dive —
(feels like a bullet point of entry.)

Tiger tiger, Blakian rage
Tell us where the war zone was
When terrorists took the World Trade
Three thousand gone in a jumpcut fade.

II
When Jessica fell down the well
(the media — the media!)
crews could not leave — they stand there still
in upside down white memory.
They were the diggers, pale and brave
die and let live, (black hole, black hole.)

And so the day three thousand died
(deafen the heart and blind the mind)
it couldn't be real — some camera fade...

love jumped from windows a hundred acres high
Broken or burned, some chose the way to go
Flamed orange sky — forever altered states — .

Like heroes lowered slowly into the well
The tired firemen dig for body parts.

Gray burning ash of hate —
God's on vacation, gambling in Reno
Long day. The families wait.

— *Claire Burch*

HELLO

Hello
I'm looking into a mirror
She was violated
Knowing my ex-wife
It was not a moving violation I was
In a strict Freudian analysis
A hickey to the Statue of Liberty
Everyone's playing bongos & guitars
I thought I heard the elevator make a remark
O Father
Do you not see encircling danger?
How is it our house has vanished
Without a trace?
Why hasn't my mother returned? How strange!
Has she taken a taste to travel?
I don't think Jews will ever be
fully accepted until we're Christian
Just like blacks will never be accepted until they're white.
I work as a freelance self-hater.
Malkuth denied
Shekinah denied
Shabbat destroyed
In unrolled fire of Torah
Unknowable violence of EL
In charge of mindlessness

One day the language
will turn against its own speakers

The power of the language is
hidden within the name
its abyss is sealed therein

This is the God that hides
that everyone sees in a book
that hides in blood
released from broken hearts

This is a blind book
not the body shattered by belief

Unseeing letters are bullets
& missiles

Visions of the Apocalypse
• Made Simple and Understandable
• A Unique Public Presentation
• Open To All

in the passage
way away from
sea, the light
takes hold of all
hands can touch
& toss as bombs
into the dark
ahead & behind

This from: Franz Rosenzweig's Star of Redemption (1918) — the
chapter 'Grammar of Pathos (The Language of Action)':

From two sides there is thus a knocking on the locked door of the
future. Life presses toward the world in a dark growth which defiles
all calculation; the soul, sanctifying itself, seeks a way to their
neighbor in the hot outpouring of the heart. World and soul — both
knock at the locked gate, the former growing, the latter acting. All
action too, after all, heads for the future, and the neighbor sought by
the soul is always 'ahead' of her and is only anticipated in the one
who just happens, momentarily, to be ahead of her. Growing as well
as acting become eternal by means of such anticipation.

Shema

breaks down the door
dead rat on doorstep
ants pouring out of his eyes

& half opened mouth
teeth sharp in grateful smile
Shemah

in dark bomb light
shatter vessels

will to die

impossible to mend

unite in light's metals
melting into flesh

praise to the One
to whom our praise is due
now & forever
creator of day & night

all embrace
life's lights
of death
entrapment's
cowl blackness

we believe more than we know
& know more than we believe

Unending is Your love for Your people
the House of Israel
Torah & Mitzvot
You have taught us
laws & precepts

day & night
reflect on them
they are our life
the length of our days
Your love

never departs
from our hearts!

I woke up in ruins
what remains resists grasp
blood saturates all it touches

evidence external
conceals what's w/in
shatter networks
skin layers in instant
corruption of metals

praise who or what or why
green stalk unfold
or mould spot spores
flower in the heat
& mix w/ death life
life death the emergency
strapped w/ plastic explosives
allusive instant of amazement

we're dead anyway
either way

to die beyond our w/in
imagined boundaries
all for the infernal Eternal

Praise the Eternal
Sovereign of
the Universe

the kids skid out of lens line
smash into unending love for Your people

who are they
are we
whose people

Let the reign of evil afflict us no more

the dot drops out of sight
no elegant turn no swift recoil
we're bereft beyond words
& words are all we're left with

You alone
are God

— *David Meltzer*

SAVAGE JETS SWORD THE SKY
HUNGRY BOMBS TORTURE THE EARTH

as for myself
I choose not to believe in war
holy or not
although I understand that it has been on
history's greatest hits list for
eons
so I tune into my own religion
          but I just don't know if I believe in
          what it is I don't believe in
          anymore

if I were Christ
I would be a drink of water
if I were Buddha
I would gladly kill myself in the garden of your eyes forever
if I were Mohammed
Mecca would be the journey in your touch
if I were a Jew
the holy land would be the covenant of my blood singing hosanna in
    your veins
if I were an atheist
I would call your every footfall god leaving footprints in the moment

each cell has memory
has soul
every chair a tree
          this is my religion:
the sacred life of the savage heart unbroken
the straight line bent by promise

no joke
I miss true friendship like I miss my hair sometimes
          no regrets
          everything in its own time
but
it's about

time
and these days
fear surrounds everyone
like a smoking halo

so for now
I just fall

falling

it's what
I do
it's what is best for
me

meet you in the fall
my friend

I fall every time
I am easy this way

— *S.A. Griffin*

JESUS POEM

If I'd been trapped in one of those towers,
and had a cell phone,
I'd have called my sister and brother
and told them I'd loved my life,
loved them, always would, and to
thank everybody for being so good to me and
to take no avenging actions,
nor support the avenging actions of others,
but to let me die with the dignity of my faith.
Then I'd step out into the air,
something opening beneath me,
the last fall of my life.
It's hard to say what I'd be feeling,
surprise, mystification, terror, glory,
but I'm sure I wouldn't be angry.
In the last moments,
there's nothing to fix,
no protest against the speed of the fall.
I imagine I'd be filled with
something beyond terror,
a feeling which is
(from where we stand)
intolerably bright.

— *Susan Birkland*

HOW TO SURVIVE AN ELECTRICAL STORM

Electrical storms tire the blood—
nightly news,
demi-truths,
the general said today this war is going to last for years,
the long slide has begun,
and where am I—
clinging to silk pillows,
waiting for rain?

At the center of my brain there is a single drop of water.

The radio announces the profligate was sainted yesterday.
I gave him head secretly last week myself.
We've all encouraged his over-stuffed longings,
stolen a little perfume when we thought no one was looking;
we have such refined secrets,
so delicately modulated you could mistake a rondo for a kiss,
a miner for a cowboy,
your brother for your death—
spitting invectives at your garage door—
it's so confusing when the radio tells you
the General and the Priest never slept in the same bed,
we can't trust brown people anymore,
unmarked letters,
and anyone named Ali.

A girl could get too scared to go outside,
but how then will I find you?
How will I remember what it felt like when you whispered
the name of our favorite saint on my wet pearl?

I've passed many days in this bleary electrified dream.

Meanwhile,
at the center of my brain there is a single drop of water.

Call it me,

call it you,
water and electricity are a dangerous combination—
fire and water mixing it up amidst the gray brain of my fear,
the gray brain of nostalgia,
the gray brain of disgrace;
I could spend my whole life worrying,
but instead I count the seconds between
thunder and lightning,
carried along by calamities' promise of rain.

The truth is,
the drop of water at the center of my brain was here before I was born,
before God had a name,
and the water loves itself,
the water loves itself,
and then again,
the water loves itself.

— *Susan Birkeland*

ON REPORTS OF THREATS AGAINST ARAB-AMERICANS

For Corey Wade
"She confided, O I hate being Middle Eastern today."

I

news kiosk owner from
Palestine, rabbi's son out of
Brooklyn, Puerto Rican
poet new to the city who never
had time to write
an old poem, son
of an Irish cop now
working at an investment
desk, cosmic dreamer, bodies, body
parts, American eyes, flags, body
bags, Afghanistan, what can we do
under morning skies burrowed
into words that will not
breath deep enough, and who
will suspend both time
and our liberties just long enough

II

Lewis and Clark move backwards
They hope to discover Washington D.C.
the Cherokee nation comes home
to the diamond-headed Exchange
John Brown rises from dust
at the foot of the Pentagon
Abraham Lincoln crosses the prairies
on a moonflooded night
Walt Whitman is confused by fire
tumbling out of American eyes
Chief Seattle dreams of Indians
dressed like clowns in a Wild West Act
Miles Davis is Dark Magus in daylight
performing for the bankers

III

I am an Arab
my feet are burning
I am an Arab
my hands are feeling
for stones that can speak
I am an Arab
with a memory
of woven sky
I am an Arab
with a Jew in my body
I am an Arab
in fear for my country
I'm Ibn Arabi
I'm the Palestinian poet
Adonis who will weep
in blue air
I'm the casbah
on clouds
and my head
turns inside out

I am a single child
raising an arm
upward toward God
or silence

I have subway dreams
and islands in my head

my hopes
are here in America
rooted to the streets
and the bison headed
emptiness at the heart
of what we face tomorrow

— *Neeli Cherkovski*

BOXCARS, NINES AND ELEVENS

A numbered event, the numbering
rising in pitch, four thousand years discordant
born of quarrel and incubated in divine
invention
— not intervention—this 911.

Arriving on the roll of New York dice
no sevens, no eight easy eight
or snake eyes (although one could infer
snake eyes by the nature of the act)
the heart is stopped by a low frequency.

There is a convergence—of luck and un-luck
of unexpected numbers: nine—representing
enlightenment—and eleven a twin
like the pair of black towers.
Chang died first, then Ang in the same bed.

The frequency was built on the Citizen's Band
around the world. In Cairo by backgammon players.
Mecca, Damascus, Qom.

By Monica in Pasadena who remembered
her groceries came to $111.11 earlier that week
and Steve whose golf score was 111.
Van Nuys, Canoga Park, Encino.

The black cloud was hookah-rich and grim
with sticky resin—
unspooling from the clerics topknot.
The sneer of the Emir—the verse of curse
the cryptic clue was: September embers.

Then the towers exploded and the noils poured down
numbered people ran screaming—

And this is how the American viewers

took it in—watching on television while their hearts
burned like rubber—waiting for news.

This was our film noire
black and white—Occidental-Oriental
melted people under concrete
the repeated penetration
of the large-bellied jet
crashing through the window
crashing and re-crashing.
But the commonplace was still common
above 14th Street.

Osama, Osama.
Bin, Bin
Atta!
Osama Bin Muhadeen
Bin Bin Atta!
Osama Bin Smith
Atta Atta
Bin Bin
Osama Bin Padilla!
Bin Bin Jones
Osama Bin Bam Boom!

Aladdin has flown
and the groundlings look up.
Listen to the xenophone notes
there is a shrill tining in the
stark sky.
The random number generator
is tumbling caged dice.
And it's coming up

nines, elevens and atomic boxcars.

— *Todd Easton Mills*

BLACK HAIR

black hair
long
wavy
or maybe recently
cut short
like your breath
as you woke
the same time as i did
on a
morning
you will never
forget
was a Tuesday
sometime before 7am here
and 10am over there

and you don't know this
nor have the time to care

but we woke up
the same second of
the same minute
sometime before
7am
to the sound of a
gasp
clogged by morning
heightened by shock
plagued by confusion

and the sound
was so much louder
than the
volume
of the t.v.
you fell asleep to
last night

but the empty room sur-
rounding you
in your bed
tells you
that gasp came from your
throat
it
knew

before the rest of you
what your eyes
would adjust to
on the t.v. screen

you rubbed your eyes like this
like i did
as they caught up to
your ears
which could hear reports
indicating
the smoke rising
from the fiery tower
was no accident

so you propped yourself up
on to your
forearms and elbows
to have a steadier glimpse
just as your belly
took control again
and pushed out another cry
through your throat
and out of your jaw
wide open
at the sight of the
tower's twin
falling
collapsing
dying before your eyes

before
"terrorism"
slipped from the reporter's
mouth
before
you had time
to catch your breath
fear
fell into your stomach

feeling weak in every joint
you went to the bathroom
to at least ease your bladder
you washed your face
your hands
poured water over your head

as your
eyes
looked dripping water
at the
mirror

my black hair
you thought

my black hair
is so long and wavy
maybe i should have it
cut short
so i will
look less like
terrorism
the kind that
reporter envisions

maybe i should
have it
cut short

like my sleep
i can't remember my
dreams
from this morning
i'm never up
this early
in the morning

and you don't know this
nor have the
time
to care

but i was on the other side of
the
mirror
i was there

you looked like my mother
tripping over
tumbleweed
in a desert
of despair

she was there
four decades
before you or i

were born
running in a
camp
as wide as fences
could hold
10,000 souls

never smiling for the
authorities' cameras
and no one knew why
not even she

at the age
of three

until she grew to the point
when she could finally see
exactly where she
had been dumped
18 years before
at the age of 2
jumping over
tumbleweed

or maybe
you looked like me
on the other side
of the
mirror
at the age of 11
putting on too much
makeup
trying to forget the
crumbles about
"Buy American"
and
"Fuck Japan"
smashed somewhere
in my shoe
about
"pick a side, girl
you know they deserved it
and
you guys
are doing it again"
and i applied more makeup
than my face could handle
as i wondered
where
will

i
be
taken
if this gets worse

until i grew to the point
when i could
drive
to the place
where
my soul
had been
concentrated
where i could
see my
reflection
in the desert sand
and
snake holes
where
i could
maybe
recapture
100,000 souls

but
the bashing and
backlashing
sent me an invitation
to see the trap
from 50 years before
that would still
be open for my long lost cousins
50 years
later
as the country
geared itself to destroy
your
spiritual homeland

maybe you don't know this yet
maybe you don't have
the time to care
but
maybe you could look in the
mirror
and see
that i am there

— *traci kato-kiriyama*

INTO THE ARMS OF ANGELS
For those who leapt from the WTC

From the terror of fire,
darkness and broken glass
on the 101st floor you step
into the clear light of day.
A quarter mile up, the wind
blows lingering smoke
from your hair, your torn shirt,
fluttering wings in the morning light.
For the briefest instant
time stands still.
In that infinite moment
you tumble into a pas de deux
with the sky, the wind
a thunderous accompaniment
filling your ears.
Manhattan gazes up,
the tear smudged face of a lover,
her arms reaching
for one final embrace.

— *Timothy Rhodes*

HIGH HAUNTS

There are countless tales of structurally displaced spirits
walking inches above floors lowered in a remodel a century before,
passing unhindered through solid doors newly hung,
stopping to weep at doors long demolished.

There is a tale of soldiers visible only from the knees up
marching through a cellar, descending an unseen slope
helms disappearing row after row, feet staying faithful
to contours of an ancient road whose buried stones
lead to a destination never reached.

No explanations can suffice for these flickering phantoms
surprised by their moment of sudden death,
random remnants of energy burned into the retina of memory
timeless, looping film images in a final scene, on a final set.

Now we build our buildings a hundred stories high
so if they tumble into rubble in seconds
will pale desk lamps continue to flicker
as ghosts pace the space between coffee machine and cubicle
will spectral lovers leap hand in hand from windows
shattered into shimmering dust a century ago?

Will a city like New York ever be still or dark enough
for any living soul gazing upward on a warm Indian Summer night
to see a thousand wisps spiralling down stairwells suspended in the sky
disappearing at the 20th floor, reappearing at the 60th
shadow moments repeating fiercely where only falcons fly?

— *Tish Eastman*

THE BLESSING OF TERROR

I am trying to write a blessing for today. I did think I might die today. I am scared of drinking water and crossing bridges.

I can see five American flags from my kitchen window.

I am trying to write a blessing for today. I am trying to be impeccable with my word, not just every word I write, but also everything I say. I do not want to scare people, neither do I want to shelter them. I only want to save them.

And writing the word not is maybe not so impeccable, and not the way a blessing should be put out into the world, but I'm concerned more with what's happening now, not with what's not or might.

Last Friday night, I was not comfortable being asked for my identification at my queer temple. When I asked what they were looking for, they said they did not know. When I asked if you do not know what you are looking for, who then will you turn away, I was not comfortable with their answer of they did not know. I was not comfortable with the announcement during the service of asking everyone, during high holidays, to look out for suspicious people during this time of heightened security. I spoke out against this heightened insecurity and my fellow queer Jews told me to keep quiet. I felt scared to be white and Jewish and wondered if, during this time of heightened insecurity, it wouldn't be easier to tell us apart from others if we wore armbands.

And I am not proud that our military has not actually lifted the gag order of Don't Ask Don't Tell but rather suspended the suspensions so that gays may now fight for America, but if they live to tell about it and if they're out, they will be punished later, after this time of heightened insecurity.

And I am not unhappy, although not is such a good way to place myself within the month of September and this life I have not chosen, but is certainly and proudly mine.

And what I love about Judaism is that at least once a year, and for some of us, more often than that, we set an extra place at the table, we heap extra food on a plate, we open the doors of our homes and our gates, and await whoever might join us. We prepare for the unexpected and welcome the uninvited. Elijah, the stranger, the wanderer is included and embraced and fed.

And what I love about America is that there is room for all of us. What I know is there is no us and no them. There is no winning. But I do not love a flag that separates me from the country I once came from and from my brothers and sisters in other places. And yes, I see the flowers and candles for Alicia, from the Mission, flight 175, we love you and miss you. In Noe Valley, I see the crayoned stars and stripes with tears, crying on a gate, for Tom, parentheses, missing. I am American, but I will not be blindfolded by the American flag. I am American, but I will not turn Elijah away when he comes knocking at my door. If we do not know what we are looking for, we will be turning ourselves away.

I am writing a blessing for today. I know the fear of the subway, of the city coming down, of being a target. And this is the blessing of terror. Being human is a life-threatening condition. I have survived being human yet one more day. I don't know how long I have left. I am blessed.

— *Thea Hillman*

THE DOUBLE DREAM OF FALLING
(for those souls who perished on 9/11)

And so we slept,
Always an ocean or two
Away from danger, bombs in
Dublin, Belfast, London and Tokyo
Just parts of the evening news, comfortable with
Dan Rather, Tom Brokaw and Peter Jennings, everything
Under
Control
That is
Until 911
Wake up
Wake up
Wake up America,
Guess what
Guess what
Guess what America,
You're part
Of the news   now
You are the
News, that obsessive broadcast,
That obsessive videotape
Repeated
Repeated
Repeated until
Numbness
Numbness set in, falling
Asleep between twin
Falling, falling between
Twin arms, falling into gray mist
Falling into gray sleep
Falling into twin
Towers falling, just
Evaporating, mist
Must be another advertising
Stunt, must be another
Artistic act, must be

Another Orson Wells' WAR OF THE WORLDS
Except this time, for television,
Waiting for the commercial break
That never came, that
Never comes, but this show just
Keeps going on, the same show every moment
Of every day, President Bush and Rudy Guliani
Stepping on the souls of the perished, stepping up
Their political careers, Rudy milking every second, every
Minute, every hour he could
With cameras flashing, video recording, always in a fresh suit,
Tie, immaculate hair-do, correct make-up,
Bush trumpeting his threats against
Ghosts whose lives went up
Against his war machine
Against his huge
Ego, against the innocents who
Paid Bush's debt, but only in
Part, Bush daily adds to his
Debt so that others will follow,
He and Guiliani became heroes
On the blood of innocent thousands
Who flew through windows, ascended to
Heaven without wings, who coughed
And screamed, who clawed for that
Last possible gasp of life,
While the fools who
Misread, misunderstood and
Defiled the Qur'an, thinking they
Were going to Heaven
Found themselves quick
In the initiatory
Flames that were but
A small portion of their
Coming Hell

But the newsmen, the young
Bouncing beat reporters, in their
Finest new dresses, sweaters, the

Somber faced anchors, each night, intoning
The same mantras, that this was a real
Tragedy, it was the first time, how
Could anyone do this, how could,
And yet the Irish in Belfast, the English at the
Picadilly Circus Station, the Japanese in Tokyo
All knew it wasn't the first time
Nor the last, that no matter how
Much America shook, they already knew
The shaking, they already knew
Their lives had been forever
Changed, but somehow,
In America, no one ever
Realized
What they'd lived through,
What friends they'd lost,
What lovers they'd lost, they
Were just part of the
Evening News on ABC, NBC and CBS,
They were just moments of an
Evening's 30 minute world coverage,
Just a filler from overseas
Without smell, without smoke, without
Blood, abstractions from a
Video, not really real, not felt
And when Guliani was voted Time's Man of the Year,
They just sighed in Tokyo, in Belfast, in London,
—they'd known it all before, but
No one in those places understood why Guliani was
Such a hero, all he'd done was step on the souls
Of the dead, used their blood for his gain,
No one understood why Bush suddenly decided he
Was a warrior, never having been to war,
But here was his moment
This would give him a chance to prove
He was a man, a man he thought,
But hollow, he didn't want to
Solve problems, but wanted to make more
War, knowing that Bush would be

Safe, but that like Belfast, war would only
Bring more death, more
Revenge, more flashing footage for the
Evening News, but little solace, little
Peace, little like the particles of
Dust that came floating,
Floating down to earth, between
The two arms, between the
Two dreams, between the
Two towers, falling, slipping down
Inside themselves
Inside the hollow ring
That now makes up our lives

— *Sam Hamod*

MY WIFE SAYS DON'T WRITE ABOUT
SEPTEMBER 11TH

For three months, I have collected facts (Elvis Presley got a C in eighth
     grade music; an average 10-gallon hat only holds 3 gallons of water;
the French writer Voltaire drank 40 cups of coffee a day)
     for a long poem dedicated to Dave Barry about the ridiculousness
of our world and our lives. After all, if our stomachs didn't produce
     a new layer of mucous every two weeks, they'd digest themselves.

But my wife—an elementary schoolteacher with a knack for pithy
     observations—has said two things this past week. (1) *Drugs have taught
an entire generation of American kids the metric system.* (2) *Don't write
     about September 11th. Period.* Recently, I quizzed my Intro to Lit class
at the university, and they *do* know the metric system, hands-down.
     These same kids, however, are more interested in learning that

the Sanskrit word for "war" also translates into "desire for more cows"
     than talking about how three planes being forced to crash on U.S. soil
affects their lives more than will a D in Psych 101 or a 4.3% tuition bump.
     It's the World War of our generation, I told them as the death count
tallied higher. The single most important event you may ever live to see.
     A straight-B-minus kid dressed as an outlaw biker (leather, chains)

asked *Will that be on the midterm?* ". . .The foxes are hungry, who could
     blame them for what they do? . . ." Mary Oliver writes in her slap-in-the-
face great poem "Foxes in Winter," which is consolation of sorts, but not
     as much as this story: Benchley's first book, *Jaws*, was nearly given
his writer father's title suggestion, *What's That Noshin' on My Laig?*
     Just today I learned Grant Wood's definitive portrait

of the straitlaced Midwestern farmer is a fraud. Byron McKeeby,
     a dentist friend, and Nan, Wood's sister, (not a couple, nor farmers),
posed in front of a farmhouse that once was an infamous bordello.
     Just goes to show that you never quite know, my wife says, then
adds that the only Beach Boy who ever surfed was Brian Wilson's
     brother, Dennis, the group's drummer, who drowned in 1983,

and I think wow, that *would* make a better poem than something
    about September 11th. I could even add in real-honest-to-goodness
headlines I've collected, like HOSPITALS ARE SUED BY 7 FOOT
    DOCTORS, BLIND WORKERS EYE BETTER WAGES, MILK
DRINKERS TURN TO POWDER, and TEENAGE PROSTITUTION
    PROBLEM IS MOUNTING, but in a week I'll learn that two

cousins and the Russian kid from my elementary school who lived
    with his deaf grandmother were all in the World Trade Center, as were
three distant relatives on my wife's side. Only today I don't know this,
    so I go on teaching my classes, feeling as if one octave of every song
I sing is in the past, waves of heat rising off the minute that came just before—
    my mind's not on lessons or explosions, but rather that at birth,

a panda is smaller than a mouse, and female canaries cannot sing.
    When my wife tells me that whatever I do, don't write a poem that gets
sentimental, I say, sure, thinking of when I first saw the ocean—from
    a lighthouse whose beacon was unlit at night, how the dunes rose
and fell like shadows of waves all the way to the water. There's nothing
    funny, I have to admit, how from a distance, the surf's thunder

sounds like static, a tv left on after every station's signed off.

— *Ryan G. Van Cleave*

NO SUCH THING AS A PRECISION BOMB

September 12th
the day after

as the talk radio venom multiplies like a virus
I feel ashamed of our only-natural reaction
we weep for our own
but care not a whit—not one bit
for the poor dark different millions overseas and underpaid
drained dry by the sweat of our shopping sprees
bombed out of history books by our Republicrat offense complex
erased from the Vietnam memorial
which remembers Roger D. Williams / Larry L. Riley / Philip G. Turner
but dis-members Tran Ngo / Dong Kiet / Heng Norodom

but as day unrolls and outrage grows my resentment folds
listening to Manhattan mothers begging for any clue
that they need not begin anew
salty rivulets cascade down smile line riverbeds carved by a lifetime of
privilege
commuters look at me
they, unashamed of my tears

but as our tears overfill the cauldron of restraint
U.S. fury bubbles up
threatening to boil over
into fleets of black steel
raining vaporized death

workers abroad flee Afghanistan
waving U.S. passports with relief
as they leave the free speechless behind
because they know
there's no such thing as a precision bomb

and our president
just back from summer vacation in Central Standard Out-of-Time Zone
where you can set your clock by the execution schedule

Bush resets his watch to the 1980s and
voila!
the Reagan administration is back and Madonna is on tour!

in Washington, hawks hunger to become vultures
feasting on the carnage to come
demands for wars of conquest
"Justice will be done!"

now when education systems fail us
we blame teachers and warn against
"throwing money at failing schools"

but when U.S. Schools of Assassins
don't do the job
like flailing fools we give them the nod
more Intelligence spending
arbitrary arrests secret evidence and
still free trips to Disney World

will we ever learn?
covert operations through the years teach us
there's no such thing as a precision bomb

for 11 months we have watched
the sick tit-for-tat of Palestinian sticks and Israeli tanks
but in our mission from god-y'know, the white blond one with an M-16
we've stabbed ourselves blind until we need seeing eye dogs
because we're only seeing eye-raqi dogs

as Israeli policy assassinates Palestinians with the pinpoint accuracy of a
Molotov cocktail party on the South Lawn toasting jobs that pay minimum
waging low-intensity guerilla war-fare-well to Salvadoran priests collars
stained red white and blue-blooded elites hand-picking Colombian
paramilitaries to savor the flesh of the poor farmers planting Cambodian
rice paddy wagons hauling off protestors who can be picked up at the morgue
formerly known as the Guatemalan presidential palace now a nightmare
visions spin past of Lebanon Afghanistan Grenada Nicaragua
lighting up Baghdad skies at the low cost of 156 personnel

darkening with the lives of 156 thousand into a decade of perpetual hell
U.S. bombers kiss Iraq goodnight every five to 10 days
for 10 years of Iraqis starving to die alive

if you reap what you sow
I fear the harvest has barely begun

acts of terror?
c'mon, we wrote the book
I have READ the book
the CIA-drafted white manual blanco which
the Department of Defense admits teaches
"fear, payment of bounties for enemy dead, beatings, false imprisonment,
and executions"

"CIA mines Nicaraguan harbors"
what a safe, sterile sentence
of death
for the poor fishermen blown to fish bait in our war against a good example

Archbishop Oscar Romero murdered celebrating Mass
graves dot the Panama Cityscape Just Cause
when Desert Shield turns to Storm
we desert our loud ideals
if the oil justifies the means

how ironic that Peter Jennings' New York terror update is
"brought to you by Lockheed Martin"
Boeing and Lockheed, Honeywell and GE don't Bring Good Things to Life
.they slash splash years of progressive policies
prohibiting export of grim F-16 reapers
F-16s reserved exclusively for civilian targets
    in regions where civil liberties
    are racing to catch up with the extinction of external enemies
    F-16s to pit Southern Cone countries clashing into arms race-ing to erase
    carefully crafted balances of power all for
    profit

    as two Hawker Hunter fighter jets bomb La Moneda presidential palace

ending generations of Chilean democracy
the Pentagon lets fly a wry smile:
"we just sold the jets, trained the pilots, plotted the course
and provided agents to oversee the coup
we didn't actually
do
anything"

if you reap what you sow
we need some new seeds
need to plant seeds of reason and outreach
saplings of civil society / acorns of Arab amiability

the point is not that this is our fault
it's that we need to stop creating fault lines

our world did not become more violent on September 11th
we just grew a little more aware of how violent we
have become

— *Paul Gandhi Joseph Dosh*

THE DAY AFTER THE CLEANUP ENDED

The trees bent
In a sort of anguished manner

The priests
The same ones

Who might have
Abused a child

Wept in sadness

And the bell

Four sets of five.

Yet none of it
Was enough

And none of it
Will ever be enough

For goodness
And idealism

And love
Have been given a solid punch
In the nose

And they have responded

Like broken limbs

Or torn biceps.

In other words, they will recover and heal
In time.

But the workers
They scream at night

And see skinless heads and arms and legs
In their nightmares

They hug their pillows
And take umbrage in their wives' arms
And breasts

But we know
Know better than they

That they will never see a baseball game

Or their children's high school graduation
Or a Balanchine ballet

The same way.

They can talk tough
About the terrorists

We all can.
But we are all liars,
Frightened to death

And somewhat in awe
Of the precision and daring of the attack

While unsure of what we did to deserve it.

The hands may have bled searching
For survivors, then the dead,
And then just body parts,

But the spirit will need the most brutal therapy

The kind ten lifetimes cannot hide.

— *Radimer Luza*

SMALL TREASURES

It rests in the hollow of her throat
Glitters like a sprinkling of stars
Repeatedly her hand finds its way
Lingers

> *His voice from the plane had been strong, calm*
> *He and others were preparing an offensive*
> *But first he needed to speak of their love,*
> *His wish that her life be lived fully*

> *Then he was gone...*

In her mind, a vision of their
Last time together
Then, as now, breeze-kissed bamboo
Cast a lacework of shifting pattern

Her hand returns to the pendant
Covers it lovingly

— *Paula Nemeroff Weiss*

MORNING RUSH HOUR, 9/28/01

*(a week after the September 11, 2001 World Trade Center terrorist attack,
in which thousands were killed)*

the toddler cries "I want Mommy, I want Mommy…"

her parents squeeze into the crowded subway car,
Daddy holding the screeching child,
who strains toward her mother

her father hands her to Mommy,
a generous man giving them a seat
the child's father struggles farther into the full car
out of the way of more passengers entering

the toddler starts sobbing, "I want Daddy, I want Daddy…"

I choke back tears of my own as I think
of all the children now missing parents,
who cannot cry out and have them return

is this inconsolable child feeling all our fear and loss
in which she is awash, and crying all our tears

the sobbing toddler grasps between the legs
of passengers trying to reach her father

"God will lift Daddy up to heaven,"
a grieving mother said, her child responding
"Does God have enough hands?"

Does God have enough hands to help us
bear our grief, to help us live compassionately,
to help us heal that gaping hole in the human spirit
that opens wherever ignorance and hate prevail?

the child's father finally wends his way
toward his crying child and takes her frantically
waving hand, "Pleased to meet you,"

he tentatively jokes

she starts to sob "I want my grandma..."
this small child, reflecting the grief
of our stricken city, this looming grief
of the ages

— *Patricia Kelly*

SURVIVING

Special days—graduations, holidays, birthdays, anniversaries
        suck the wind out of you. And the wonder of everyday events,
        munching popcorn on the sofa in front of the TV, a walk in the
        park resonate with emptiness.

Unfinished—plans pounce from unexpected corners.
        As you pass the cologne counter, a whiff reminds you
        of the present you bought—but didn't give. A friend's
        chatter about a cruise resurrects the memory of the trip
        you planned—but never took.

Reality—requires a pep talk each morning, in order to start
        your day. Like a mantra, you repeat, "That was then, this is now,"
        how ever many times it takes to get you
        out the door and through the day.

Vivid—memories play non-stop, like old movies
        through your mind. A sunshine-filled vacation at the Shore,
        the engagement ring and will you marry me,
        the secrets only the two of you shared.

In—the privacy of your home,
        where no one can hear, you scream,
        "Why?" And allow the wild person within
        to rant at the powers that be.
        Demand answers—Now!

Vulnerable—you stand naked before the mirror,
        look for signs of life. Instead you see dark circles,
        worry lines, sallow skin, and empty eyes.

Intense—emotions flood over you each time you realize
        that you no longer can say,
        "Remember when?"

Nothing short—of a tragedy, you think. But
        catch yourself, and remember.

A tragedy would be never to have had them.

Going forward—you straighten your shoulders,
    repeat the words that you read somewhere.
    "To live in the hearts we leave behind is not to die."

— *Pat West*

TIME AND PLACE: 11/11/01

At almost 88 my father finds the times
confusing. Not the wake up, show up on time
times, though he sometimes loses track of lunch
because my mother is no longer here
to make sandwiches and soup, but the times
he's going through now. It was confusing this fall,
a whole week without baseball, commercial
television without commercials, and
real-time coverage of stuff you'd rather not see,
beginning with those planes and buildings. Time was
when he knew exactly what was up and how to act
and he's got the hardware to prove it, a Silver Star
and enough German shrapnel deep inside
to set off an airport warning,
in these nervously calibrated days.

Newspaper maps sit neatly folded on his desk,
a good sign my brother says, that Dad's not disengaged
from everyday life. But they are only cartographies
of confusion for a world that has changed too much.
Names have been altered and the old boundaries
are hard to find, and some countries aren't even
there. "I can't find Taliban," he says,
"on any of these maps."

— *Neil Nakadate*

WORDS, LIKE SURVIVORS

It's like Pearl Harbor, some people say...
> Yet those were soldiers at their post.
> Perhaps betrayed by readiness,
> but not imagination.

Some say, it's like the London blitz...
> Yet with no sirens, no warning cry,
> no shelters to wait out the hell.

Some say, at last our time has come
like Belfast or Jerusalem,
or other targets 'round the world.
A pipe bomb here, a school bus there,
a daily dose of outrage.
String the "incidents" end to end
somewhere, someone's being mourned.
Somewhere, someone's mourning...

> Yet with audacity, horror grows.
> For every gaudy monument
> (built on stone, or built on hate),
> size does matter, in the end:
> Ground Zero breaks new ground.

Some say, it's like a movie:
an action movie gone insane,
jumping off the summer screen.
Demonic villains. Clichéd plot.
The special effects. The spectacle...
> Yet in such movies, every time,
> the fate of victims is white noise
> as Arnold, Wesley, Bruce, or Chuck
> slaughter foreign foes with glee.
> "Stars" and "extras" here trade place.
> The cartoon heroes never were.
> The victims are as real as us—
> despite a cast of thousands.

Some people say these things, and more.
About spirit and self-sacrifice—
vigilance and courage—
the beating of the nation's drum—
even the death of irony...
> Yet all the words leave me unmoved.
> Words, like survivors, won't be found
> buried under pride and rage.
> In time, we are compelled to choose
> what to say, what to silence.
> But for now, the forever now,
> I can't see beyond the tears.
>
> I only believe the tears.

— Tom Guarnera

A BLESSING FOR NEW YORK

God bless this magic city
this peninsular pentaboroughal big-apple magic
this welcome-the-whole-wide-world Ellis Island magic
this torch-toting harbor-hostessing Statue of Liberty magic
bless this

bless this fabufashionable Madison Avenue magic
this Broadway off-Broadway off-off-Broadway magic
this gritty roller-coasting Coney Island hot dog mermaid magic
this Disney-bedemoned neoned big-ball-dropping Times Square magic
bless this

bless this slow-mo multi-alphabetical subway train magic
this knish thin-pizza bagel (it's the water) egg-cream magic
this Knicks Rangers Giants Yankees yes-even-the-Mets magic
this finger-snapping Frank Sinatra king-of-the-hill
            (more like a mountain) magic
bless this

bless this water-towered roof-flowered 24-hour magic
this horse-drawn blanket-lawned imagined-on Central Park magic
this bridge-suspended tunnel-underwater ferry-back-&-forth magic
this Renaissance Gothic Art Deco skyline (minus the Twins) magic
bless this

bless this magic city
this Yahweh Allah Dios God magic
this Chang&Eng Laurel&Hardy Captain&Tenille magic
this inseparable inseverable *love, love will keep us together* magic
this one-world-under-God indivisible with liberty and justice for all
            magic

bless this magic city
bless this magic city

bless this
bless them
bless us

— *Marj Hahne*

NEW YORK MEMORIAL

My world has become a moving collage
of American flags and makeshift memorials
Thousands of candles and flowers laid fresh.
The dead are mourned
Our country is praised
And this New York girl just wants to go home.

I cry for the heroes, the everyday people
I cry for the love outpouring from all
I cry for the city now buried in ashes
I cry for the lives impacted forever.

Six days before the tragedy struck
I flew home safely, New York to L.A.
With notes for the poems I was going to write
—now changed irreparably, innocence lost—
About beautiful vacation, family and friends.

The California sun seems too bright.
It pierces my tears as I pass another shrine
of mylar balloons and messages of solidarity.
I write a check for disaster relief
but my arms ache from the distance I try to breach:
3000 miles. I stretch across America
To hold those I love
To hold those who lost loved ones
To hold strangers.
I want to comfort people whose paths
    so recently intersected mine.

This New York girl just yearns to go home:
I should be clearing debris
Searching for bodies
Singing in subway stations
and writing a poem for every life lost.

— *Meredith Karen Laskow*

STRANGERS

I didn't know the man in black pants
who plunged headfirst
from the top of the north tower

or the young mother trapped
behind a locked door
on the eighty-seventh floor.

I never met the couple
crushed in their final embrace
and stuffed into one body bag,

or the fire chief quickly buried
under tons of concrete,
steel, glass, and ash.

Nor did I ever say hello
to the blond woman
who called her husband to ask

what she should tell the pilot
standing beside her
at the back of the plane.

I never shared coffee
with the six-foot-four executive
who said, "If we're going

to crash into something,
let's not let it happen.
Our best chance is to fight."

Yet I have felt sun on their skin
and tasted wine on their lips.
I have run using the long muscles

of their legs and felt air

rush into their lungs, their hearts
pumping in my chest,

and they have combed my hair
each morning, tasted
cereal from my bowl,

and held my children in their arms.
At night they have watched
stars shimmer through my eyes.

Now they have returned
to earth and air, but I still feel them
stirring inside me, walking

the long corridors of my brain,
searching for something
irretrievable, precious, still there.

— *Lucille Lang Day*

EVEN NOW

Into my witches' brew, communal cauldron,
everything goes.
That's how I travel the world from my kitchen:
quiche, lasagna, curry, sukiyaki, stew
moving across continents in my cauldron,
offering not my will
but my surrender
to the mix.
It's the day after
and all I want to do is cook,
invite my friends over for a feast,
celebrating life.
Boil and bubble, toil and trouble,
the pot spits in fits, and asks me this:
What if the everyday is even more sacred now?
What if the kitchen where we gather
is a tiny tucked-away sanctuary of the soul,
where burnished pots and orange bowls
speak the wonders of the world,
and what if meals together are not just time-tested recipes
or modern-day experiments but benedictions
to honor our hunger and our quenching of it,
and what if the oven is not just heat
for the common cook's convenience
but the healing, purifying fire of the sooty soul?
If I can't heal the world, at least I'll cook
a good brisket, my grandmother once said,
so I throw the spirit of my ancestors
into the cauldron, doing both.

And with each boil, the steam sends up its question:
What if the simple meal on the table—
a quiche made with homegrown onions,
chicken simmering in cardamom curry
lasagna smothered in cheese and garlic
beef braised in soy sauce, sending its salty bloom
out into the air—is not a meal but a kind of blessing,

a Zen *koan* asked of monks in a mountain-top temple,
or the frayed parchment of a prayer
slipped between stones at the Wailing Wall
and all the hands clasped in church and steeple,
and points between?
What if each dish is the universe's open palm
inviting us to feast together, celebrate, partake
and return the cook's magic by sharing it.
This is what we know to be true.
And so, the day after
we gather for a meal marking the end of this season,
traveling to America, France, Italy, Israel,
India, Ireland, Africa, Arabia and Japan at our table,
making of this meal a universe,
even now,
called "home."

— *Leza Lowitz*

9.12.01
TWIN TOWERS

Formal announcements
Instructed people to stay put
Stay put
The threat was limited to the other tower
When met with more announcements
And other cautions to stop or return
Went back up
Went back up
On the 48th floor they heard the
Announcement
They heard the
Announcement
That the situation
Was under control
Several
Got in
The elevators
They heard the
Announcement
That the situation
Was under control they heard the
Announcement
And went back up they heard the
Announcement
And went back up they heard the
Announcement
Towers
Towers
Twin Towers
We're going to be fine
We're going to be fine
They told each other
As they grabbed
Their
Pocketbooks
Their
Pocketbooks

— *Laurie McKenna*

SHANKSVILLE, PENNSYLVANIA, OCTOBER 21, 2001

At our Somerset motel, Gary,
reddish-brown hair, big grin, says,
"Good thing you came now.
A few weeks ago we were all rented out—
forensic dentists." We're here

for orchards, walks in leaves,
antiques. I hunt blue glassware,
you, old radios. To get
to Route 30 Antiques,
we drive through Shanksville.

A plane fell here. TV doesn't show
a hand drawing a shade in a farm house,
grief-gaunt faces lying in bed at night.

On this plane, people knew
no magic hand would pull them
to safety. A man had called his wife
from the air. The last words she heard were
"Let's roll!"

Falling
over 500 mph
near heavy-bearing apple orchards:
jonathan, ida-red, delicious. The road

winds to an open area
near the small business district:
cardboard, crepe paper, wire,
hand-written words "for our fallen heroes."
Several locals around it as we rise
and fall on curves of hill

out of town. Forty days. A shared history:
explosion, loss.

They can't drive away as we do.

— *Kenneth Pobo*

SHE SMILES ON THE TV SCREEN

looking like all those tough girls I knew in school
hair bleached a little too blond, her face lined and sad.
Her husband was up there on the 92nd floor,
just a stockbroker with lots of kids
an Irish man who loved to dance.
She talked about the first time they met
seeing him from the back, she liked
what she saw and wanted to see
if he looked that good from the front.
The plane hit the building below him.
He called her on his cell phone.
praying a rosary as he talked
working his beads, she said
till there was silence.

— *Karen Karpowich*

VOLUNTEER

The fires at Ground Zero stopped burning today.
It's the week of the winter equinox.
Cameo Christian's face is round, her eyes wide.
I stare into them, not able to escape the sadness.
She's been at the Disaster Relief Center for hours.
We talk.
Her hands and my hands are flat on the table.
Mine appear steady, hers shake.
I've practiced my words, knowing
not to promise what can't be delivered.
I wonder if Cameo has practiced her despair.
A Spanish speaking man is at my left
next to him a redhead from the Upper East Side
a broker, a school teacher, a short order cook.
It's hard to separate the aid seekers from the givers.
We are all on the edge of something
New Yorkers who never look one in the eye,
never touch a hand, never risk a prayer.
So many billions of dollars in aid, so many
particles of dust and ash.
A cold wind has come in from the North.
My face is dry and chapped.
Cameo's eyes are wide.
In the end she asks for so little.
The folding chairs we sit on
have such hard backs.

— *Karen Karpowich*

TIME TO DIE — SEPTEMBER 11, 2001

He called to say he was stuck at work.
There was just no way
He could come home early today.
Maybe, he wouldn't come home at all.
It might be never.
He said, a little catastrophe
Has just happened to me,
And to all the people in the offices here
TODAY!
Bow your head and pray.
The ceiling is starting to cave in.
Out the window I see a fireman.
But, he can't get near.
There's too much fire and smoke in here.
I think we've been hit by a bomb.
God, I wish I could come home!
If I never see you again, I love you.
Yes, I know you love me too.
I'm busy now, Goodbye.
I'm sorry, I have to take time to die.

— *Karen Elizabeth Harlan*

21ST CENTURY

Sweltering sadness in this woeful world,
multiple murders already as a teenage girl,
i was the accomplice to some,
few hundred bucks and a day of sadness
just to have fun,
i'm stunned to see
the people we be,
losing life by chopping trees,
is it really resolved
just by planting a few new seeds?
Destroying the biosphere,
making the world bleed,
please feed the fallen foes
of unfortunate followers
of lying leaders, guilty governments,
wasteful war lords, too cheap to afford
donations to caring causes
that cure the ailments of our earth,
unwanted births,
i use self control
instead of birth control,
cuz 315 dollars ain't worth your soul
like common said,
you don't know it but that was
my heart you just bled,
the search for disintegrated people
with no trace of even a limb,
jumping off of burning buildings, rushing wind,
fallen fears, flailing arms, trying to swim
to a quick death, instead of melting away,
running away,
Hell is where they'll stay,
from fire, from heat, suicide?
but i would probably do the same,
free falling freedom, a sudden splat
splitting soul from body,
blood,

brains splattered skull
from a 12 gauge shotty,
if violence is forbidden in religion,
why has more people died
in God's name than from anything else,
terrorism exists because of noble causes,
don't you think they have reason to strike without pauses,
but the masses are blinded from the truth
and we end up with millions of losses,
how can the u.s. think that we're everyone's bosses,
the world's police,
cuz of that we'll never find peace,
the suicide bombers won't cease,
unless jews give palestinian land another lease,
so please, know the facts, relax, why be racist
if the best race might be latino, asian, or black,
cut those with less some slack,
let's make a common pact,
teamwork, so my shit might stop getting jacked.

— *J.Y. Ho*

GATE 6A

(After 9/11)

The *danse macabre* begins at dawn,
the cleaning of America,
Workers check in at airport security
to scan for infamy or purity.

Citizens scan immigrants.
Immigrants scan citizens.
Immigrants scan immigrants.
Christians scan Jews.
Jews scan Moslems.
Moslems scan Hindus.
Hindus scan Buddhists.

Buddhists scan scanners.

Faiths of renegades,
creeds of missionaries,
credos of schoolchildren,
purple hearts of soldiers,
elusive ghosts of pasts and futures:
the human spirit scanned
at Gate 6A at the San Jose airport
by electronic wands of fairy god scanners
at the threshold of paranoia.

— *Judith Terzi*

NASEEM

Mommy, I'm scared
The Twin Towers collapsed
We're in the college basement. It's dark.
Students and professors are crying.

Mommy, I'm scared
It's my first day
I don't know anyone
We've been here for hours
I can't eat, I'm not hungry

Mommy, I'm frightened
We must evacuate
There's a crack in our building

Mommy, I'm terrified
There's ash and debris everywhere
I'm walking home
There's no transportation

Mommy, what shall I do? I'm lost. I'm lost.
Oh, the dead bodies
the bodies,
the—

Daddy! How did you find me?
    I prayed, my sweet. I prayed.

— *Juanita Torrence-Thompson*

ASK ME NOW

for edward sanders & peter gold

standing at the finish line
of the boston marathon
in the middle of april
when americans pay their taxes
under penalty of seizure
or imprisonment,

thinking about the harbor
where our early patriots
dressed up like natives
& stormed the british ships
to throw overboard
the hated crates of tea —

on this patriots day 2002
at the end of a long & difficult run
let us rededicate ourselves
to the freedom & justice
our ancestors intended
when they founded this nation

& fought here in boston
& throughout new england
for the freedom of our country
& the right to govern ourselves
for better or for worse,
however imperfect or misguided,

o let these truths be self-evident,
that we shall be free to worship
as we see fit, that there are many people
& they have many different gods,
that what may be fit for you
may not work for me,
but let us live in peace together,
& let us share our riches

with those who have none,
& let the future of our nation
be secured by the intelligence
& creativity, by the compassion

& commitment of our people
to the future of humanity itself
& all people everywhere
who toil with us here on Earth
to make a living
for ourselves & our families,

to enjoy the fruits of our labors
no matter where or for whom
we may toil, to enjoy the pursuit of life,
liberty & happiness
in the many disparate courses
it may take

as we exercise the freedoms
guaranteed by our constitution,
to be free from armed invaders
in the comfort of our homes,
free to say or believe in
anything we may want to,

free to enjoy the substances
our happiness may require,
free to meet & mingle with our friends
whomsoever they may be,
free to dance & sing,
free to make love with whomever we please,

free to have children
or not have children
as we may see fit,
free to live outside the dictates
of conventional society
like true americans,

open-minded,
humanitarian,
tolerant of the differences between us,
quick to accept,
slow to anger,
loath to harm or destroy—
so let the word go forth
from boston today: yes, let us rededicate ourselves
to the freedom & justice
our ancestors intended
when they founded this great nation

— *John Sinclair*

THE NEWS OF NOVEMBER 1, 2001

The news is some maple leaves are still clinging.
The news is blue sky, and two guys
going through the neighbor's dumpster
for some good scrap.
The news is the deep cadmium yellow
of those leaves. Is primary colors.
The news doesn't care if I didn't believe
in bombs, if I come out as a total
bomb atheist, if I come out
against the Christ of the Bombs,
if I decry religious medals bubblegummed
to thousand pound "Bunker Busters."
The news is today, the first of November.
It's Sixty degrees, the breaking news
is a cerulian and aqua marine sky
and I can't take any more visions
of the Twin Towers. The news
of the bombing is, there's more bombing.
The news is tree limbs lit
by the south-inclining sun. The news is
I'm here, shielded by my skin,
with my heart and lungs and endocrine
glands, with my sins of omission
and sins of commission.
The news is we haven't set up
concentration camps
for the Arabs' own good—so many
getting beaten up in the Bronx,
in Queens. The news is
you'll go to your death if the cause
is right. The news is aspirin.
Is last night I couldn't sleep,
my legs were twitching, is we have not
had carpet bombing since Viet Nam,
is no need for defoliation in this other
corner of Asia. Is afternoon raging
with its blue skies. Is a few clouds

coming up, is me in my chair,
pen and notebook. Is pen and notebook.
No news is no news.
The news is a sneeze, a sudden chill,
the disconnected dreams at the onset of a cold.
Is it leads to more news.
Is mainline addiction—TVs with
the sound off. My friend, Carei, having
a tooth extracted this afternoon, and he
on Cumadin. Is you, wherever you are,
reading this. Is you in the St. Patrick's Day Parade,
in your green pants and green shirt, drinking
green beer. Is afternoon, the TV off,
I'm breaking into a sweat for news.
The open back door, a dog down the block,
the news is all local.
Cars pass as they did yesterday, as the day
before, as the bombs fall, as the scratch
on my wrist from a rusty nail continues
into the history of red. Is nothing I can say.
Light glowing through the trees, refugees
eating grass without benefit
of an extra stomach. The news is serendipity
and gunsmoke. The thump of a bomb,
an ammo depot going up. The news is
there's an unidentified threat. The news is
be alert. The governor's whereabouts
unknown. Terrorists are among us,
he says, you don't want to advertise.
The news is he tells us to live
normally: go shopping, go out to eat.
The news is I had soup for dinner
and am in my chair. Night has fallen.
News is we need more trumpets
about now, a whole new brass section,
some reeds, a dynamo on drums,
a chorus of angels—I mean it—
the news is, it's another day. The sky
stayed calm and bright from here to Gaylord,

from Gaylord to St. Cloud. The city traffic
was bearable. For once I went through life
uncomplaining.

— *John Minczeski*

SIMPLE POEM FOR A DIFFICULT TIME

I carry my daughter of six weeks
Strutting with the bombast a rock star
Fresh from electrifying Madison Square Garden
Seventeen thousand disposable lighters thrust aloft
In demand of my encore

This immense pride stems
Not from the radiant beauty of my daughter
(Though she is both radiant and beautiful
Clearly I can take genetic credit for neither)
But from the fact we have just completed
With only minimal thrashing and wailing
A successful mid-day diaper change

And so as I strut
I thump my chest like a gorilla
And blurt loud a mutually agreed upon favorite line
From one of our mutually agreed upon favorite authors
I am the Lorax, I speak for the trees!

My daughter smiles with the dazzle of a thousand suns
The impish crinkle of her mouth
Enough to urge middle-aged men
To tear off ties and dig dirt with their fingers
To plant gardens of chrysanthemums and gardenias

But though I'd like to believe
My daughter of six weeks
Capable of cogent analysis
Of not only every Seussian couplet
But also every Shakespearan sonnet
And Poundian canto
The most up-to-date research concludes
She has no idea what I'm saying

Thus her delight cannot trace
From the profundity of the content

Of I am the Lorax, I speak for the trees!
But must instead result from the resolution
The firm conviction
With which her father her pronounces it

So it is with dismay
I hand my daughter to her mother
For I know I did not write the line I spake with such conviction
Nor am I truly The Lorax
But just a high school English teacher
And though I recycle when convenient
And sometimes even when not
The sport utility vehicle in my driveway
Seems proof enough to attest
I hardly speak for the trees

Since that moment
I have wondered if there is anything I do speak for
As passionately as The Lorax
Defends his forest

It is only now
While the debris of this horror still smolders
That I know what I want to say to my first child

In the wake of airplanes crashing into icons
In the shadows of skyscrapers
Collapsing upon themselves
Like too heavy lopsided cakes
In the face of people leaping 100 stories
And suffocating in stairwells
In the face of all that
I want to tell my daughter
Being good matters

Lifting people up instead of stepping on them—matters
Holding hands instead of clenching fists—matters
Calling a stranger a friend instead of a label—matters

Stopping at stop signs
Returning wallets without rifling through contents
Waiting in the regular check-out line with more than 15 items
Letting people merge in front of you in traffic
Waving when other people let you do that
Waving, in general
Listening
Recycling
Voting
Giving blood
Telling the truth
All matter

In the face of the horror we've witnessed
In the face of all of it
We can stand up and love

I want to tell my daughter
I cannot promise I can keep her safe
But I can promise to be kind
And to love wherever and whenever I can
And I hope one day
She will never have to sit in a high school auditorium
Listening to a poem like this one
After people have died
In crashed planes and toppled buildings
And I hope the world we will rebuild
Will allow my daughter to believe
The thing her father once told her
Being good matters

— *Jeff Kass*

"WHEN MY BROTHER AND I BUILT AND FLEW THE FIRST MAN-CARRYING FLYING MACHINE, WE THOUGHT THAT WE WERE INTRODUCING INTO THE WORLD AN INVENTION WHICH WOULD MAKE FURTHER WARS PRACTICALLY IMPOSSIBLE," REMARKED ORVILLE WRIGHT IN 1917

how to name this horror
what *language*
can do anything but fail before it?
an official at my son's school
suddenly discovered that a
woman colleague
was on one of "those planes"
(with her two children, one five, one three years old)—
began simultaneously
to weep
and to curse.
Terror: "intense, sharp, overmastering fear"
and Anger
not that it was done "here"
but that it was done
at all
Hideous official language
issuing out of the government and
the television
(there is no difference between
the government and the television)
hideous actions
numbing us
What is the relationship
between the "public poet"
and the "private poet"?
Does such a "relationship" exist?
Is it possible to say anything
and mean it
at the same time—

I mean
something real (like death)
Can we respond
to the reality of their death
with any reality at all?
They were, and
they are not—
and their martyrdom
was as horrible as any horrors of war
Everyone knows this
"I have a friend," a friend writes,
"I phoned...left messages...."
And the leaders who comfort us
seem nearly as fiendish
as the fiends
who planned this horror
This is a day
of mourning
mourning for
deaths
but mourning
for our own
burned innocence,
our own burned selves—up in flames!—
for all the selves we murder when we cry "VENGEANCE VENGEANCE
VENGEANCE"
mourning for the sweetness
we pretend
each day / may
harbor:
this is a flower
for New York City
for all those
who died
and, dying,
live.

— *Jack Foley*

"President Bush asked a receptive Congress to grant him unprecedented powers to wage a war against an unidentified enemy, seeking authority to annihilate not only those responsible for Tuesday's attacks, but those who..."

YOU ARE TOO HUMAN

You are sitting in the cockpit
Behind you dozens in panic
In front of you a building
Approaching you rapidly
Your noble sacrifice
Your sacred act of courage
You will be dying before this thought is complete
You are not afraid

You are sitting in your office
Your report is at the printer
Your boss will be proud of you
You smile
You're thinking of calling your wife
You said unkind words to her this morning
You look out the window
You see an airplane
You run, you run
Your heart is in your neck
      Your ears
           Your eyes
Beating, beating, alive
You cannot comprehend
You will never again speak with your wife
Your unkind words will remain
Bitter memories of love

Eleven of your friends are gone forever
It's your day off
But you go to the station
A few women are sitting on a couch
Their boyfriends, husbands, brothers missing
Quiet conversation masks the tension
Your tears are ready
Tonight, in your wife's arms,
You will cry inconsolably
Your buddies clench their teeth
Harden their faces
This is not a place to be human
You see so much

You are so alone

You are at home
A little fever, nothing major
Your wife is at her new job
Your children in school
You are not used to being home alone
You turn on the TV
Casually, somewhat restless
Your wife's workplace is on fire
Incredulous, you look at the people
Jumping, escaping the fire

You are walking down the street
Your hear footsteps
You turn, facing the eyes of
A young Arab-looking man
It's dark, but he looks nervous
Is he on his way to plan the next attack?
You are scared
You will not let this happen again
You reach for a knife in your pocket

The sense of security
In the country you are serving
Is shattered
You have not had much sleep
Your body is aching
You ignore it, as always
You have decisions to make
Reports appear on the fax,
            The computer
                    The phone
People walk into your office
Constantly impinging on your irritated tiredness
No real news
You want action
How will you decide
What is the right thing to do?

— *Miki Kashtan*

EXCERPTS FROM SEPTEMBER 11, 2001

I praise the firemen: truly as heroic as the antique gods,
as Whitman said. Medics, too: divine messengers of mercy
indeed. And I go to each and every one killed or wounded
by terrorism as tenderly as "The Wound-Dresser"
made his rounds in Whitman's Civil War poem,
as devoutly as the firemen's beloved chaplain
who was hit in the head and killed by falling debris
while administering the Last Sacrament
to victims fallen to the sidewalk at the foot of
the doomed skyscrapers. I think of all the victims
and their loved ones with immense compassion
and also mourn the two ancient giant standing
Buddhas of Compassion destroyed by Taliban artillery
in Afghanistan six months before the twin Towers
were destroyed in Manhattan—destroyed ungently,
unlike Tibetan sand paintings scattered by their artists
as a meditation on the ephemerality of art and life.

That being said, I say the following:

Chicken Little said "The sky is falling,"
but on 9-11 the sky*scrapers* were falling:
a million tons of steel and glass rained down.
Environmentalists had been called Chicken Littles
for sounding alarm over a hole in the sky over Antarctica
and Greenhouse gases heating up the planet's atmosphere.
Weren't those skyscrapers doing to the Biosphere
what those terrorists did to those skyscrapers?
But Greenpeace hangs banners from buildings;
it does not blow them up. This poem is the banner
I hang in the air above the still-smoldering skyscraper ruins
and from every skyscraper on the planet still standing.

A nonstop convoy of dumptrucks took
the obliterated remains of those twin skyscrapers
to the Fresh Kills landfill on Staten Island. Staten Island

where Antler & I read with Allen Ginsberg in April '90
and afterwards took a tour of that stench-exuding
New York City dump. Allen died 4 1/2 years ago
with the arch-example of the "endless Jehovahs" in "Howl"
visible in the distance. Yes, the Empire State Building
was visible from his deathbed window. His 1974 poem
"Jaweh and Allah Battle" is still right on the button
of the Cain&Abel/Isaac&Ishmael history of the Middle East
and of the human species in general into the mists of time,
the grotesque penchant for humansacrifice to Moloch.

If only Allen were still alive to help us figure out this ongoing Planet
    News scoop he had
such a bead on for decades: i.e. what on Earth is going on
on Earth? He saw right through all national/international chicanery.
His 1965 poem "Who Be Kind To" invoked that 2001 would be
"the year of thrilling god," not the year when deranged Philistine
    Davids
sling jetliners into skyscrapers that "stand in the long streets like
    endless
Jehovahs" &/or Allahs. His "Jaweh and Allah Battle" lays bare
the "High Noon" showdown folly of two "Chosen People"s squeezed
into the same tiny Holy Land who squabble which one holds the
    deed, which one was
loved more by their mutual ancestral patriarchal bigdaddy.

Pity the poor innocent people diving into the cool air
    from the inferno forcing them out the windows.
Pity the poor innocent humans burned by a hell
    created in the human brain. Pity the poor affluent
    innocent humans burned alive and crushed like flies
    between the layers of the arch-cathedral of Commerce.
Pity the poor innocent know-not-what-they-do people
    caught in the inexorable karma of the god of Gasoline
    enshrined and worshipped in the temple of wailing Wall Street.
Pity the poor innocent people trapped and doomed in the
    larger-than-its-father progeny of the Imperialism State Building
    up which the Natural World climbed with humanity in its hand
    while U.S. Air Force planes tried to shoot it down

causing the Natural World to plummet to the pavement
—the Gorilla species close to extinction a mere half century
after the RKO plane circled the planet before
the opening credits of *King Kong*.
Pity the poor humans trapped and doomed inside the twin progeny
of the Empire State Building that soon overtower'd
the Chrysler Building that Lorca cried out from the peak of
decrying Rockefeller's poisoning of the Hudson River.
Pity the innocent bystander minions of Rockefeller crashing
an oil-laden *Exxon-Valdez* into pristine Alaskan shores.
Pity the poor commuters sardined into the twin Molochs
that punctured a hole in the ozone layer and was planning to crash
a half billion two-car garages through the Great Wall of China.
Pity those innocent accomplices aboard those skyscrapers
rammed into the sky sabotaging the atmosphere for the entire
    planet.
Pity the poor reality TV hostages cowering in front of their televisions—
their favorite commercial-riddled soap-operas/sitcoms/gameshows
pre-empted by the bad news not everyone buys Madison Avenue—
cowering in front of televisions where this terrorism gets reported
but not the terrorism of Global Economic Godzilla.
Pity the poor people who died for Rockefeller's sins.
Pity the poor people who died for Hitler's sins
that caused a Zionist state to be imposed on Palestine.
Pity the souls who were snuffed because Commerce rules
rather than an interfaith ecumenical spirituality to foster
compassionate harmony among all the peoples of the planet.
Pity the poor humans trapped and doomed inside the karmic
bull's-eye of the nature-blind cyclops on U.S. Dollar.
Pity the poor children seeing this on their TV screens
even more violently psychologically indelible than
the exploding Space Shuttle. This explosion hit home
more than all the explosions in movies—more than
the White House blown up in *Independence Day*.
This Pearl Harbor struck at the end of the summer
Hollywood launched a movie version of *Pearl Harbor*.

A mere half century before T.R. waved his pre-nuclear Big Stick
at the rest of the world,

Whitman's "Salut au Monde" imparted a planet-embracing blessing
    from America to the world:
        I salute all the inhabitants of the earth...
        Good will to you all, from me and America sent!
        My spirit has pass'd in compassion around the whole earth....
        Toward you all, in America's name,
        I give the sign of democracy.

Damn the terrorists for provoking a tidalwave of flag-waving,
for making the flag factories work overtime,
for reintroducing the bill to ban flag-burning,
for making Winston Smith love Big Brother even more,
for increasing likelihood Bush will be re-elected in 2004,
for unifying the country around the Son of Desert Storm,
for intensifying the threat the Alaskan Wildlife Refuge will be
    drilled rather than expedite transition to non-fossil fuels,
for putting Global Warming on the back burner,
for putting the Rainforest Holocaust on the back burner,
for distracting attention from Population Bomb terrorism
    fomented by Vatican rather than Taliban,
for riling up chauvinism in America despite Ferlinghetti's
    1958 warning that nationalism is "the idiotic superstition
    that would blow up the world."
Damn the terrorists for following the example set by U.S.A.
    at Hiroshima and Nagasaki.

The first "skyscraper" was only 130 ft. high,
built on Manhattan in 1870 when land began running out on the
    island
the Dutch bought from the Indians for a mess of glass beads.
The Woolworth Building babel'd 60 stories heavenward in 1913.
The Chrysler Building 77 stories in 1930, from the top of which
    Lorca
shouted out his warning about planet-raping skyscrapers
just before the Empire State Building was built:
    Now there's no one to mourn the wounds of elephants.
    There are only millions of blacksmiths
    forging chains for the children to come,
    There is only a mob of laments

unbuttoning their shirts in hope of the bullet
and dark nymphs of pestilence scream.
—the Jesus Chrysler Building that crucified the Biosphere,
from the top of which Federico Garcia Lorca wept
over the New Jerusalem and the New Golgotha,
and wept over the New Roman Empire's gunboat diplomacy,
and wept over the Hudson River "drunk on oil" vomiting into the
        bay
above Staten Island where New York would come to accumulate
one of the largest/foulest mountains of stench-exuding garbage
in the world, to which the debris of the World Trade Center
would be trucked 70 years after Lorca wept over the New Rome
from the top of the Chrysler Building:

> *I denounce the people*
> *that lifts its cement mounds*
> *where the hearts of animals beat,*
> *where we'll all tumble down*
> *in the final merrymaking....*
> *I denounce the conspiracy*
> *of these office buildings*
> *that don't broadcast agonies*
> *and that erase the jungles.*

If still alive, wouldn't Lorca denounce skyscrapers that don't
        broadcast
agonies of a half million Iraqi children killed by U.S. Embargo since
        '91,
or the fact the lush rainforests crucial to the continuation of life on
        Earth
have been vanishing a football field per second since the 1980s?

The oil-driven war against the Earth known as the Industrial
        Revolution
crashed into the Ozone Layer that protects the Earth from the Sun,
and the karma of America's getting drunk on oil for over a century
crashed into skyscrapers like a drunken-driver into World History.

What if Black Elk in his old age, instead of converting heartbroken
to Catholicism and waiting heartbroken on the reservation
for John Neihardt to write down his heartbreaking story,
what if, instead of weeping on Mt. Harney, Black Elk had taken

flying lessons from Orville Wright and what if he had tried to fly
a biplane into the Empire State Building soon after it was completed
in 1931, to protest the U.S. Calvary's genocide of the Indians
and Buffalo Bill's genocide of the buffalo to make the world safe
for McDonald's? ...

In October '67 Ed Sanders tried to levitate the Pentagon
with levity, not with explosives or an airliner full of jetfuel.
Yes, Ed and an army of hippies surrounded the Pentagon
like the ghosts of Ghost Dance past, except they wore peace-paint
rather than warpaint, and attempted to levitate the Pentagon
with Allen Ginsberg's "Pentagon Exorcism"
and the Egyptian Book of the Dead. A flower child
daintily stuck a flower's stem down the rifle barrel
of one of the ring of soldiers poised between the
five-sided symbol of war and the flower-arm'd hippies.
Contrast that gentle image of potent flowerpower
to hijackers crashing an airliner into the Pentagon 34 years later
like Slim Pickens riding an A-Bomb in *Dr. Strangelove*.

Whitman took his stand at the tips of peninsulas
    and on the peaks of high-embedded rocks
to cry "Salut au Monde!" 75 years before Lorca
took his stand at the top of the Chrysler Building
at the southern tip of a peninsular island
    called Manhattan,
and shouted out danger, shouted out warning—
shouted a warning to Guernica and Warsaw:
    The Luftwaffe is coming!
    The Luftwaffe is coming!
shouted a warning to Hiroshima and Nagasaki:
    The Manhattan Project is coming!
and shouted out a warning to America and the World
    about the Hudson River getting drunk on oil
    40 years before a U.S. river caught fire
    and 58 years before a million gallons of diesel fuel
    went down the Monongahela.

Where is the hero who can transmute

this hellish fate into a heavenly destiny?
Joseph Campbell, pray for us! Huston Smith, pray for us!
Alan Watts, Meher Baba, Sufi Sam and Allen Ginsberg, pray for us!
Rumi, awaken us to our dervish planet spinning toward the brink!
Shalom Salaam! Salaam Shalom! "Peace!" in Aramaic
and Esperanto! "Peace!" in all the diverse languages going extinct
amid the "Buy! Buy! Buy!" lingua franca of the Madison Avenues
of the "limited time only" "going out of business" clearance sale
of planet-devouring Mega-consumerism!

Calling all avatars of compassion! Inspire pity on suffering humans
but also on the one-eyed lion and no-nose bear in the Kabul Zoo!

Oh let Rumi lead the dance to where
the Kaaba and the Kabbalah lie down together!

Oh let Rumi lead an army
of ecstatic pacifist dervishes
spinning like hejira gyroscopes,
spinning so fast all possibility of violence
is lost amid the need to maintain centered balance.

I take my stand on the tip of my tongue
and on the tip of my heightened brainlobes
to cry: *Salut au World Peace!*
        Salut au World Joy!
        Salut au Monde O Poets to Come,
        annunciate with angelic tongue!
        Salut au ever-expanding love of this
        beautiful precious endangered planet!
        Salut au Peace in every language
        that ever evolved in the human skull!
        Salaam Shalom! Shalom Salaam!
        Shalom Salaam! Salaam Shalom!"
                AH!   OM!

— *Jeff Poniewaz*

8:48

It was 9:08 when a coworker told me
A plane had struck the World Trade Center
He could see a small fiery
Photo on the net
I am ashamed to say
I was upset
Over a petty work issue
And thought there had been a
Minor accident. Yes,
My thoughts were on myself
It was 9:11 when other coworkers started
Talking, milling around
Still, no announcement was made
Soon we heard that a second tower
Had been hit
No announcement yet and
We had to work
It was 9:27 when I realized that one of
My two best friends no longer works at some
Other building downtown
That her new workplace, her new job
Is at Tower One
And I called and I called and I
Called her office number but
Nobody answered and
The rings were the loudest, most
Disquieting sounds I had ever heard
It was 10:10 and still they wanted us to work
Though everyone I neared in the halls
In the bathroom in the pantry
Shook his or her head
In disbelief in horror in slow motion
It was 10:23 when I had
The presence of mind to call this best friend
At her home and was thrilled though terrified
To hear her sobbing to hear her
Ragged voice

To hear her
Tell of being a few blocks away and
Seeing it all, and
Seeing and hearing from no one in her office
Though she had been calling and calling
And she lived just ten minutes from work
Had thought that was a blessing
Now she did not know
What had become of her coworkers.
Some had become friends in
The last three months
At her centrally located new job
At my office we were not yet told
To go home and it was 12:30 when
I went out to lunch. On the midtown streets
I saw armies of
Workers: white, blue,
Pink collars
Aged young in-between
Scurrying shuffling dazed looking up into the sun
Fearing more planes?
I wanted to join them
I wanted to walk keep walking walk away
I wanted to join my two best friends
My man
My cat
I didn't even know then that
Another friend in Brooklyn has
An ex-boyfriend who worked in Tower Two
We had doubled-dated, gone to Great
Adventure Amusement Park
I didn't know to be scared for him as I was for all the
People I didn't know and
For myself, too, even though I wasn't on site
And still I couldn't lose sight of the fact that
We had to keep working though how could we
How could we edit words that now seemed to fall off the page as
We would later learn people were to fly try to fly off the towers?
Finally at 2:04 we were told by voice-mail to

Take off if we had personal things to attend to but
How do you attend to the death of
Thousands of people you do not know and to
The possible death and near death of people you do know
And to the destruction of your stupid innocence along with a
Landmark building, a symbol?
How do you return to work
The next day at 9:00 because
Otherwise it will be a personal day and
You do not have the time for a personal day?
Who has the time the time
The time: it was 8:48?

— *Iris N. Schwartz*

TWIN

In double-pained dread, I wait my turn. Doubly afraid
of the vaporized bodies and the venom spreading violet.

An eye for an eye. Am I next on the altar stone?
Fear of planes and neighbors, a double helix of terror choking

memories from the ashes of another disaster spawning hate
on the playground with Jerry Anderson red

in my face, screaming: Traitor, traitor, hostage-taker!
Ayatollah, Coca-Cola, Drop dead, Turbanhead...

I give him a black eye and feel better.
An eye for an eye. Glass towers shatter. Answer: Flatten

villages near Kabul. Twin replies, two sides of the same fate coin.
It has always been so. From when the Tigris and Euphrates

drew dual lines in the sand, twins laid tip to toe form a circle,
a cycle, history's gyre where above the burning tower, the falcon

Cannot hear the falconer.

Khoda-ya, save me from the fork-tongued snake. How dare I?
My limbs, my loves intact while twin towers entomb thousands.
        Guilt

settles in the bone and one fear is martyred for the other.
I trace the Braille on my gold pendant. The script rises in Arabic
        flames
to one unfailing response. La ilaha illa Allah, There is no god but
        God

— *Haleh Hatami*

BE AFRAID

Doesn't look old enough to shave, this gun toting,
badge wearing defender of our freedoms.
ID please, he says, no smile, eyes tight, black leather
shined, polished, menacing.

No, I say, not in your purview of acceptable questions.
ID or arrest, old man, said with ferocity unknown just
a year ago. No, I repeat, the constitution forbids
your asking. If you have nothing to hide ... he says.

I won't let him finish. Let me see *your* ID, the one
with *your* home address and Social Security number,
I say. No, says this armed intruder. If you have
nothing to hide, I say, and he puts cuffs on me.

— *Johnny Gunn*

THE NEW YORK POEM
for Jan Foster

I sit in the dark, not brooding
exactly, not waiting for the dawn
that is just beginning, at six-twenty-one,
in gray October light behind the trees.
I sit, breathing, mind turning on its wheel.

Hayden writes, "What use is poetry
in times like these?" And I suppose
I understand when he says, "A poet
simply cannot comprehend
any meaning in such slaughter."

Nevertheless, in the grip of horror,
I turn to poetry, not prose,
to help me come to terms—
such as can be—with the lies, murders
and breathtaking hypocrisies

of those who would lead a nation
or a church. "What use is poetry?"
I sat down September twelfth,
two-thousand-one in the Common Era,
and read Rumi and kissed the ground.

And now that millions starve
in the name of holy war? Every war
is holy. It is the same pathetic story
from which we derive
"biblical proportion."

I hear Pilate's footsteps ring
on cobblestone, the voice of Joe McCarthy
cursing in the senate, Little Boy exploding
as the whole sky shudders.
In New York City, the crashes

and subsequent collapses
created seismic waves. To begin to speak
of the dead, of the dying ... how
can a poet speak of proportion any more
at all? Yet as the old Greek said,

"We walk on the faces of the dead."
The dark fall sky grows blue.
Alone among ash and bones and ruins,
Tu Fu and Basho write the poem.
The last trace of blind rage fades

and a mute sadness settles in,
like dust, for the long, long haul. But if
I do not get up and sing,
if I do not get up and dance again,
the savages will win.

I'll kiss the sword that kills me if I must.

— *Sam Hamill*

SOMEONE SAYS
THEY LOOKED
LIKE CARTWHEELING
BIRDS

the quietest moments some
one will say are the worst.
Someone doesn't know what to
do with new wedding photos.

Someone eats, not tasting
what she swallows. Someone
who just got her law degree
went home to the rooms she

would lie in alone, can't
imagine looking for a job
now, watches a video of
the wedding weeks ago,

how handsome her husband
looked, how "we wish you
a lifetime of happiness"
on a card now stings. Some

child says the falling birds
were flame birds

SOMEONE GOES OVER
OLD LOVE LETTERS

someone forgets for a
moment, thinks of
going next door to
borrow—then falls
apart. Someone
still expects a
woman with

strong arms
coming back
with groceries
and a joke. Some
one waits for a
black Honda, thinks
of the smell of coffee.
In another house,
someone starts to
make lunch but
there's no one to
make lunch for.
She can't stop
seeing the
shapes tumbling
from the sky.
Someone sets up
an altar with
incense and a drawing.
Her child stops
before it, says "come
eat dinner Daddy"

AFTER SEPTEMBER 11

one child writes words
with plastic letters,
brings them to an altar
with a drawing of
his father. Look,
Daddy look. Someone
who used to talk to
her mother kneels near
the fish tank, still
sees her car in the drive
way, talks to the fish

now, tells them it's just
us, Sarah is gone

AFTER SEPTEMBER 11

someone keeps calling
his answering machine
to hear his voice even
as the building is burning,
is stunned in days to
hear: "this number is no
longer in service." Some
one cancels a deposit
on a new house, a trip,
a life, can't eat pistachio
ice cream and not
remember. Someone
hugs a pillow, still smells
cologne of someone
missing, can't make her
self move his coffee cup
from where his lips
last touched it

SOMEONE SAVES
THE LAST 8:41 E MAIL

"Tuxedo for wedding
September 11, 2001—
don't forget to get
measured, the account
is under my name."
His friends save the
message to their hard
drive. His other says
she's glad he had so
many happy thoughts
in his last moment.
His fiancee could not

look at the message
for many days

SOMEONE RE-PLAYS
THE E MAIL

how good the bachelor
party was. Another keeps
happy news, "a 75 dollar
win from a football wager.
Somebody pays all phone
bills just to be able to hear
her brother's voice, "that
is all we have left of him."
Someone wishes she'd
saved instant messages,
his last one, "I love you,
Karse." Another looks at
an e mail signed off at
8:49:35, says it's like
watching someone die

SOMEONE SAYS HIS
OFFICE WAS ALWAYS
FILLED WITH FLOWERS

plants and roses
and in his house. His
woman stood among
them watching the
leaves burn across
the harbor. Some
one says he was
sprinting toward the
fire, helped others
at first, the last
anyone saw he was
headed to the towers.
Someone says "if

I had been there
with him I couldn't
have been able to
stop him from doing
this. It was a passion
to help"

SOMEONE SAYS
SHE GAVE ME VISION

someone says his last
words to his wife
were "Everything
will be ok." Someone's
last words were to his
father, "don't worry,
Big Guy, it's all
under control." Some
one said his friend
enjoyed life, fit a lot
in during his 37 years.
Another says her big
brother was always
there to protect her,
doesn't say he was
her twin, born one
minute earlier, always
there and now, not

IT WILL BE OK

honey, my mother
always said when
something seemed
scary. Ok. Honey.
Always. I'm strong.
"Honey, I'll be ok,"
the last words on
a phone tape from

the tower on an
answering machine.
On another answer-
ing machine, "Ok.
yes, we're highjacked
and they've got
knives. I love you. It
will be ok and good
bye" from the man
trying to convince,
with his "honey,
listen it will be
ok be ok"

OCTOBER 18, 2001

Mist on the pond,
his blue eyes sky.
Jeweled grass. I
think of my mother's
bedroom vanity
buried in Johnson's
baby powder, snow
thick, deep enough
for a box of money
to be camouflaged in
it. Footprints trailing
powder thru the
house. We wore masks
clearing the house out.
Talcum in drawers,
in shoes, in cashmere.
How today it would
be evacuated

OCTOBER 15, 2001

news of another
hijacked bus. Lately,

after I pet the cat I
turn on the news for
the disaster de jour.
In Dupont Circle
last night 3 beggars
spitting and snarling,
"got a knife— you
be my deer." Every
one's walking a tight
rope and, as if to
mimic those cart-
wheeling birds, the
ones jumping from
the burning towers,
falling and crashing

IN THE ONE TREE OF
SINGING BIRDS
after Sept 11

I never saw them, it's
like a boat made of
birds. Sycamore maybe,
long thin leaves. Past
crows and geese, like
crystals in a grey house
or stained glass on a
morning nothing seems
bright. I never see the
birds, maybe too many
to see one as one, a
hill of feathers, a beach
ball of singing, the
only thing I can't see
but believe

OCTOBER BIRDS

not the cart wheeling

birds of fire, bodies
flaming in circles
from the top floors,
a tree of birds, loud
and bright. Eve tells
me of days with her
mother, how she
is escaping, a kite
without any string
and I think of my
mother's last days,
yelling that the one night
nurse was a murderer.
After ballet, a startling
blue sky, stunning
as the day the planes
tore holes in it. Or
today's headline
"Capital shut down"

AFTER A WEEKEND
after September 11

of blackness,
each stab of
news, only
bad, a
swoop of
crows. I was
not hungry,
ate cookies,
wild for some
thing sweet
and slid into
the dark of
a film, wanting
to escape, not
think of the
next trip, the

last months
the days
losing light

OCTOBER 29, 2001

yesterday, the
twisted faces on
tv, ground zero
memorial. A
woman who
couldn't speak
without sobbing,
"I wanted to
breathe him in,
I wanted him
to be inside
me. I wanted
to tell him he
has to help us,
get us thru. He
has to help
his daughter,
his brother, his
sister. He has
to be inside me,
fill me, help me"

OCTOBER 29
   After September 11

another wildly
bright clear blue
day. Cloudless
except for the
shade, the huge
dark inside. A
cloud seeded
with poison, a

black hill of ice
that stains what
ever moves near,
wild bright and
crisp, the nicest
fall except that
it's this fall

OCTOBER 29, 2001

wild and bright
like that Tuesday,
September. Not
a cloud, nothing
not ordinary. But
today all the rusty
oaks, their leaves
burnt sienna. What
has always been
there, spilling
across for the
geese, a blaze
against a concrete
sky like those in
front of a firing
squad or on the
105th floor of a
doomed building
about to leap

OCTOBER 29, 2001

I can't think of
Riti's baby blooming
only wonder how
she must hold her
belly with each
wave of news.
Inside, he's

safer. Her diamond
glittering in her
nose, her smile
rhinestones. The
news, a miscarriage

OCTOBER 30, 2001

When I leave the
house, the cat's
found her spot of
sun near the orange
tree. I'd like to
curl into myself,
I could imagine
lying down beside
her. Last night
when I couldn't
sleep, on CNN, a
plastic tent for 4
where you could
live for 4 days,
escape gas and I
forget what else.
What next, October's
mantra tho the oaks
glisten in flame and
the geraniums are
exploding in
gorgeous nail polish
red as if nothing
could stop them

— *Lyn Lifshin*

IN THE AGE OF GRASSHOPPERS

A grasshopper with a roomy apartment building
for a stomach
tiptoes around the edge of the world.
It would take forty billion dollars to feed, clothe,
provide good water and sewerage systems,
basic education and medical care
for every man, woman and child in the world

The grasshopper army on its hind legs
looks like a grinning radiator grill
355 billion for defense
100 billion for a war no one wants
against a beautiful land and its ancient people
bin Ladens and Bushes in the Carlisle Group
turning hefty profits for the last twenty years

You never heard grasshoppers devour a field?
You never heard the crackling of houses
split like match sticks, children
with swollen bellies and big eyes
looking at you when the crops go down?
Have you heard the whining language of insects
eating until no one is left & nothing standing?

But they always leave a little, don't they?
A little left over to work the machine
through the plague of locusts, the rain of blood
In the age of miracles a doctor weeps
as he recounts the marvelous plastic surgery
he was asked to undo on an insect woman
without a mouth. They had sewed her lips shut,
layer by layer, and left a small round hole

for a straw, so she could eat, left a monster
as a living example to the others. The doctor wept
at the healing art perverted to instill raw terror
Scratch any insect in the Carlisle Group

see if blood comes out
or is it ancient dust, the bones of bloodsuckers
radiator teeth chewing arms and legs
like garbage compacters because they can't stop eating
because we let them, because they can.

— *Janine Pommy Vega*

HOLY SMOKE

Taking Tuesday back
or removing the black figure
from the constellation of Karma
would only condemn us to experience
again and again the time loop of history
as in the relentless barrage of TV sets
in a world without an audience.
"There is something in the air," you said
dreaming of a plane crashing into
the twin towers of Nostradamus,
nor was there any security when you took
your flight back across the Atlantic
a week later.
a shudder in the loins engenders there
the broken wall. the burning roof and tower
and Agamemnon dead...
Walking up the stairs the fire fighters
could not put out the fire from the heavens.
Black smoke encircled the crowns &
the heat passed even Dante's depiction
of the Inferno's daily routine.
What is the way to true Reconciliation?
What is it that we must reconcile
to break the chain of our own making?
How to lure the Lightbringer back to Paradise?
Don't expect answers from the man with the bullhorn.
Ask the Shambala Masters or David
Carradine, the Kung-Fu champion
Remember Bamiyan & the blown up head of Buddha!
It will take detachment to detach.
Attachment will only take us straight into the trap,
there where all the bullion lies buried
below the 3,000 dead.
P.S. The money goes through Switzerland.

— *Ira Cohen*

I SEE AGAIN

the sixty-year-old man
forty-eight hours tired
walking from hospital to shelter
a picture in his hand,
Have you seen this man?
have you seen my son?

On the other coast
safe in the kitchen
my four-year-old son
plays with football figures
six inches high. Takes the helmet
off one and puts it on another.
Talking all the time.

I listen to his nonsense as if it were
the secret to the universe.

Nahnaaaaaha boo boo
You can't catch me.

I see again
a tower flame into flower.
A single body falling.
You can't catch me.

Tackle! he shouts
with little boy fierceness
crashing the green team
into the red.

His eyes sparkle. His skin so smooth.
My heart lurches at the thought
of losing him.

In New York, the man drags
a wrinkled hand through

his shock of hair, *Have you seen
my son? have you seen his name
on any of the lists?*

Tackle! my four-year-old's forehead
furrows, his hands clap and toss the figures up.
They do not puncture, they do not shatter
as they fall.

I see again the silhouette.
Body black and spinning down
blurring past the glass.

My son's brow clears.
He straightens one helmet
that has gone askew.
He hums a little tune.
Safe? Are we safe?

*Mommy, can I have
some juice?*

He looks at me up
from between his lashes.
I nod. I cannot move.

I drink him drink him in.

— *Gail Ford*

DIE TODAY?

> *I hear it on the news.*
> *He says, "My wife called on her cell phone. Hijack.*
> *I turned on the news. A plane hit the Pentagon.*
> *Hers."*

If I knew we would die today
what would I do?
Not the laundry. Not the bills.
Might take my husband and son
to say goodbye to all our friends.

I would meet everyone
eye to eye and touch them
on the hand. I would keep my husband
against my hip, and my son's head
nestled under my chin.

I wouldn't die in bed.
Outside. The beach.
To stand on grains of sand
shifting under our feet
the salty air against
our eyes and cheeks.

I think I'd talk a lot at first.
Then slowly quiet. Sit
the three of us together
me between my husband's knees
back against his chest. Our son
folded in my lap.

All three of us looking on
the turn and wheel of gulls
the rise and curls of color
the sand, the sky, the sun.

I hope that we would breathe together,
the lift and letting go of the rising, lowering sea.

Maybe the tide would take us.
Maybe the sand could cover us
and time would press us down
press us into the ground
like leaves between pages
in a book. Maybe
much much later
tectonic plates
would press us up
and someone passing
tossing rocks
would find us
the three of us in rock
arms around
and holding on,
the three of us
motionless
biding time
together beside
the rising
falling
sea.

— *Gail Ford*

BACK THE NIGHT BEFORE,

I yearn for the huge silver airliners to pull backwards
out of the buildings they've rammed into.
I yearn for the bullets to return to the guns,
for the knives to retreat from the flesh as if

they had never thought of entering,
that the knives return to their box-cutting,
with no move to the left or the right.
I plead with the explosions to return back into their bombs,

their hand grenades, their mortar shells, back
into the airplanes filled with fuel for the long journey home.
I plead that the mile upon mile of rubble and broken stone rise
back up into the buildings they had been before the attack,

the roads back into being, leading again to the homes of loved ones.
I beseech the blood, the pieces of flesh, the eyes,
the internal organs, the skin, the organs of love-making
to float up from deep in the rubble and soil

and weave themselves back into the
living bodies of family and community.
I cry that we gain the determination to climb
back before the deathly events, back the night before,

the night of September 10th, where everyone
is talking to each other and listening to each other over dinner —
how to live fairly with each other, how to live fairly with the planet —
the next day the same people climbing onto the same airliners,

flying successfully to their destinations, the balance of things
swinging back toward the center, minds flooding
with visions of a new century just begun.
I reach my hands up toward the sky and plead

that cooling rain fall down, that a bright moon rise
into the black sky, that all the stars are luminous against the

backdrop of darkness and that the families are all safe and
home again, that the only fires are in the fireplaces and in the stars.

— *Skip Robinson*

FOURTH OF JULY

We are on a friend's balcony
across from the U.N.
it is the 4th of July
we come here every year
to watch the fireworks
it is like watching them in
your own
backyard
or almost like on tv
last year there was a dense fog
so we only got to see
the dense fog
lit up
like profuse columns
of thick billowing
gray smoke
tho if we would have
watched it on tv
we'd have gotten
a whole different
take
angles being what they are

what i like best is
to turn my head
left
from time to time
&
watch the explosive light
as its reflection
bends
& folds & melts
the glass on one particular
building
across the way

this is the first fireworks
since 9-11

& the biggest ever says
Macy's
it will be punctuated by
a moment or 2 of silence
& 2 columns
of light

tho angels are non-existent
their images
appear
everywhere

my wife is very nervous
the threat of terrorism
has been shoved
down our throats
all week
by the gov't
& media
alike—
to me
this in itself
is an act of terrorism

anyway we're drinking
eating
talking
& waiting

one of the cops
at a check point
on 43rd
knew just where
we were going
when i offered my i.d.
& said we were headed
for a party in Tudor City
"April's" he laughed

good naturedly
"or their neighbor
next door"
"Maybe April's" i replied
"but most likely next door"
& walking away
turned & shouted
"if you get there by 8
we'll save you
some barbecue"
really wanting to
chide him & his
comrades
for not looking in
my wife's
tiny bag
which could have
after all
contained a small
explosive device
or a detonator cap
to say the least

to set off one of those
"dirty bombs"
she's always so worried
about

9:40
they've begun
we stare & stare

into the blitz
awaiting some sign
i start this poem in my head
stare left a couple of
times
stare right
a few times
at the three huge

industrial chimneys
expecting their
imminent implosion
& collapse

i've been thinking
all week about that
& the possibility
of the fireworks themselves
being sabotaged
& of course
about dirty bombs going off
but not being able to reach
us way up here
& all week she's been saying
that they have a five mile
radius
& me only being able
to reply
that's radius
& not height but that
if we're meant to die
at least we'll be
among friends
& that she can stay home
if she likes
but that if it's written that
her time has come
she'll
die
anyway
even if she stays in the
house sleeping
on what will be a very very hot
evening

when the fireworks conclude
i think about how
they are one of the few
completely democratic

things
we all share
& how essentially the moment
of silence
tonight
was a dud
along with the whole
spectacular show
my wife says
a bit tipsy
"was that it?
will there be
more?
that wasn't much of a finale."
"that's it" i quip
"i thought it was just me
but you felt that way
too."
"yes" she says
then begins to ask others
they all unanimously agree
that the biggest
light show ever
was nothing
more than a twinkle
in a flock
of angels'
eyes

— *Steve Dalachinsky*

FALL

the flags were only able
to climb half way up their poles that day,
the sky was unbearably heavy
and nobody had anything to say—

i pray for oxygen masks to fall from the cloudbursts
because i'm tired of breathing the sadness in air,
apartment complexes like haunted houses
because we live in fear,
ghosts in the washing machine,
the sobbing faucet is all i hear.

tv sounds off battle cries,
angry like leaves in the fall,
some people held hands hoping that somehow
it was easier for two to fly,

but they just fell
like lovers leaving the world behind
bailing themselves out of hell
because god wasn't about to help,

and what would i do if life
threw me a sudden curve
and fireballs were pitched at my home plate?
my poems fate—
fahrenheit 451.

all i can do is give blood;
call my loved ones?

say, "mom, i know i haven't lived up to your expectations
and didn't always score my goals, (i only hit the post),
but at least i gave them a try—
and when i held your hand
i always felt like i could fly,"
because we always say cheesy things
in those situations.

i'd finish with,
"i love you,
tell dad and amber i love them too,"

and "thank you,"
because if i only had two words to tell her
they'd be thank you.

and if i only had time for one,
one lonely word—

i wouldn't say anything,
i'd grab the oxygen mask

and inhale.

— *Michael Cirelli*

SALEM HILL HYMN SING

The Angel of Death is abroad in the land,
only you can't always hear the flutter of its wings.
—*Winston Churchill, 1944*

A screaming comes across the sky
like a low-flying jumbo jet. Crescendo.
Decrescendo. Same old thunder
and I can't remember why
the books are all about revenge
but they are. Old people singing hymns —
What a Friend We Have in Jesus —
no wise cracks, not a derisive twitch
in the room. Christ almighty, what a pal.
Heckman and me, seventh grade trombones —
Jesus puts his money in the First National Bank.
Jesus saves. And Mike Malone across the street
drilling out the center of a sawed-off broomstick,
black powder packed in to make a rocket.

All the books are about revenge
because when your beloved uncle dies
someone goes through his attic trunk.
Not even his wife knew he was grand wizard
of the local Klan, white sheets and pointy hoods
carefully folded. Now they're singing
On a Hill Far Away, The Old Rugged Cross
while crazy Tom talks about that time
he beat the holy crap out of some queer.
Tom, the kind of crazy everybody laughs at
and loves — the cops told him, Yeah man
we know where you're comin' from
but there's laws now to protect these people.

Lorraine, bless her oceanic heart, rings in
like a temple bell to bless the notion of two men
exchanging vows to sanctify their union.
She walks away, and all the way home Tom's

behind us on his Harley, 140 miles an hour
in a white hood, flaming cross
on his handlebars like a branding iron,
God's truth screaming in the night,
crescendo, like a low-flying jumbo jet
down Cresson mountain where white neon
screams ridge to ridge that JESUS IS ALIVE
maybe living somewhere in Argentina,
maybe Dr. Mengele's next-door neighbor.
And still I'm trying to explain to everyone
not listening, not even in the room anymore
that the emblem of suffering and shame
is me, and all the books are about revenge

— *Michael Schneider*

TIME CHANGE

Thoughts between after midnight and before dawn
Arrive suspended in stillness
Without sleep and dreams, restless, coming on the cusp
Of daylight savings and standard, only to fall back, fall back.

For half way through this Autumn season
Since September, we remember
Everyone has said, all agree . . .
The world of late indeed has changed
Is not the way it used to be,
And perhaps for this time being I seek escape, need relief
Finding comfort basking in the emptiness of silence and the quiet dark,
For warmth, pulling the covers over my head, hiding.

It is my wish to retreat
From the attacks of morning headlines
To avoid confrontation
And the conflict of conversation,
Yet all the while, awaiting the promise,
Which is the first sound of bird song
Signaling the end of the night
Just before the break of day.

And amidst soundlessness, still a smile
My heart fervently opened,
With hope that under a new sun,
Arising and enlightening
Surely, someway, somehow, somewhere
May reside, renew, and radiate,
What would become the gift of truth,
A way to be clear
Closer freedom, justice, and peace,
A true course toward answer and solution
Our world and peoples nearer harmony.

— *Charles Pappas*

Biographies

Opal Palmer Adisa, writes what writes her. Sensual, sassy and sensitive are words that best describe her. She flirts between the breaths of laughter. She mothers, teaches and writes full time and manages time for friends and play. Her forth coming works are: *No Regrets*, a novel, *Caribbean Passion*, and *I Name Me Name*, poetry collection.

Antler is the author of *Factory* (City Lights, 1980), *Last Words* (Ballantine, 1986) and *Selected Poems* (Soft Skull, 2000). When not wildernessing or traveling to perform poetry, he lives near the still wild fringe of the Milwaukee River in Milwaukee, Wis., where (surprisingly considering the boldness of his work) he was recently named Poet Laureate.

RD Armstrong (Raindog to his friends) writes when he isn't working on the *Lummox Journal*, or publishing one of the *Little Red Books*, or producing a CD for the On The Record series, or working on someone's house. He also runs a poetry workshop and maintains two websites. Visit him on the web at http://home.earthlink.net/~lumoxraindog/. As I said, he's a busy guy.

Eva Yaa Asantewaa writes about dance for The Village Voice and the New York State Council on the Arts. She also maintains a private practice in Tarot-based counseling, meditation instruction, Therapeutic Touch, and other holistic modalities and has taught widely for many private and community organizations. Her poetry appears in *The Zenith of Desire: Contemporary Lesbian Poems about Sex* (1996), *Does Your Mama Know? An Anthology of Black Lesbian Coming Out Stories* (1997), and many other print and online magazines. She has performed poetry and trance meditations with drummer Bernadette McGowen and has often collaborated with dancer-choreographer Nadine Helstroffer. Her poetry collection —Your Weight on Other Worlds — needs a publisher! Read *Dancing World*, Eva's eNewsletter on Tarot, psychic and spiritual development, and creativity at www.yahoogroups.com/group/DancingWorld.

Cathy Barber has an M.A. in English from California State University, Hayward. She is a writer of both poetry and prose. Her work has appeared in *The San Francisco Bay Guardian, Occam's Razor, The Crazy Child Scribbler*, and online at *Tattoo Highway*. She lives in San Mateo with her husband and two daughters.

Coleman Barks is a poet and Professor Emeritus of English at the University of Georgia, Athens (1967-1997) Retired. He has written many books of his own poetry, most recently *Tentmaking*, Maypop 2001 and *Club: Grandaughter Poems*, Maypop, 2001. He is world renowned for his translations of the Persian poet Rumi. In 1995 Coleman appeared in an hour long interview with Bill Moyers on the PBS special, *The Language of Life*, and again in 1999 with Bill Moyers in a special called *Fooling With Words*.

Daniel Berrigan is a catholic priest, social activist, and poet, born in Two Harbors, Minnesota, USA. (brother of Philip Berrigan). His book of poems, *Time Without Number* (1957), won the Lamont Poetry Award. Active in opposing the Vietnam War, he went with professor Howard Zinn of Boston University to Hanoi, North Vietnam, to assist in obtaining the release of three American pilots (1968); the diary he kept during this mission, along with 11 poems, became *Night Flight to Hanoi* (1968). With his brother, Philip Berrigan, he gained national attention for destroying draft registration files in Catonsville, Md. (1968); in 1970 he was sentenced to three years in prison for this, but he went underground for several months until federal authorities arrested him on Block Island (off Rhode Island). After 18 months in prison, he was paroled in 1972 and participated with his brother in the first Plowshares Action (1980), a protest at the General Electric Plant at King of Prussia, Pa. Living among Jesuits, writing and conducting retreats, he was arrested regularly for his protest actions at weapons manufacturers and other sites (1980-92). He wrote over 50 books, including *The Trial of the Catonsville 9* (1970), an autobiography (1987), and at least four films.

Susan Birkland is a writer, performance artist, and drama therapist. She has been living and working in San Francisco Bay Area for 17 years. She was born in Minnesota and lived in Texas for 23 years. She has been performing in and producing music/poetry events all over San Francisco forever, it seems.

Shepherd Bliss is a Vietnam Era vet, farms in Sonoma County, and recently contributed an essay to the book *Shattered Illusions: Analyzing the War on Terrorism*. He can be reached at *sb3@pon.net*.

Claire Burch is a writer and filmaker. She is the author of *Stranger In the Family* (Bobbs Merrill), *Homeless in the Nineties*, *What Really Killed Rosebud?*, and *You be the Mother Follies* (Regent Press). Films include *James Baldwin*, *Street Survivors*, *Ghost of the SF Oracle Meets Timothy Leary*, and, most recently, *Chelsea, Cobra anf the Infamous Bones*. Articles have appeared in publications such as *Life* (Special Report), *McCalls*, and *Saturday Review*.

Kenneth Carroll's poetry and plays appear in *Black Literature Forum, Konch, Role Call, Weavings, In Search Of Color Everywhere, Spirit & Flame, Bum Rush The Page, Potomac Review*, and the *Next Frontier*. His short stories appear in *Gargoyle*, and *Shooting Star Magazine*. His freelance writings appear in the *The Washington Post*. His book of poetry is entitled, *So What: For The White Dude Who Said This Ain't Poetry*, 1997 Bunny & The Crocodile Press. He is executive director of the award-winning program *DC WritersCorps*, and teaches creative writing at Duke Ellington High School for the Arts in Washington, DC. He was awarded a 2002 literary fellowship from the DC Commission on the Arts and Humanities.

Neeli Cherkovski's latest book of poetry, *Einstein Alive*, will be published by 1 Gauge Press in the fall of 2002. Pantograph will publish *Toltec Stone, Mexican Windows* early in 2002. He is writer-in-residence at New College of California where he co-directs the MFA in Critical Inqiry.

Michael Cirelli garnered much respect and little money in the Bay Area performance poetry scene. He has been an individual finalist at the National Poetry Slam and has toured the continent featuring in front of packed venues from the Nuyorican Poet's Café to Vancouver, BC. He currently lives in Los Angeles and will be teaching poetry workshops as part of Poets in the Classrooms sponsored by PEN West.

Allen Cohen lives in a basement apartment in Oakland, CA where he receives improbable impulses to save the world and celebrate life. He is the author of two books of poetry and the editor of the *San Francisco Oracle Facsimile Edition* and author of the CD ROM *History of the Haight Ashbury* and going further back in the time machine one of the founders and editors of the original *San Francisco Oracle* and one of the originators of the Human Be-In.

Ira Cohen is strictly intergalactic and has no time for bios. If you want or need to know more about him look in a crystal ball and iracohen.org, bigbridge.org, and mysticfire.com. His latest book from Panther Books, NYC is *Poem From The Akashic Record.*

Robert Creeley was born in Massachusetts in 1926 and graduated from Black Mountain College, one of the centers of American artistic ferment in the 50's, where he befriended Charles Olson and edited *The Black Mountain Review.* Publications include: *For Love* (1962); *Words* (1967); *Pieces* (1969); *The Finger* (1970); *St Martin's* (1971); *A Day Book* (1972); *Thirty Things* (1974); *Away* (1976); *Later* (1978) and *Memory Gardens* (1986). He has also written prose, including *The Gold Diggers* (1954/65) and *The Island* (1963); as well as essays *A Quick Graph* (1970) and *Was That a Real Poem* (1979). There ia a *Collected Poems* and *A Collected Prose* and a *Collected Essays* available. He has written, "Why poetry? Its materials are so constant, simple, elusive, specific. It costs so little and so much. It preoccupies a life, yet can only find one living. It is a music, a playful construct of feeling, a last word and communion" *(Selected Poems 1945-1990).*

Steve Dalachinsky is a longtime friend and colleague of many great New York poets, from Jack Micheline and Gregory Corso to Lou Reed and Richard Kostelanetz. Steve Dalachinsky and his wife Yuko live only blocks from where the Trade Towers went down. Describing his own highly respected work, which has been published in dozens of literary magazines, he says it "consists of minimal editing & tries to combine descriptive & transformative elements to create a language of seeing & almost unhampered sound." He often reads his work to music in the New York clubs, and has a CD called *Incomplete DirectionS* produced by The Knitting Factory. He is also the author of several books of poetry, including *The Final Nite, In The Book Of Ice,* and *Blue.*

Diego Davalos: "I am an Ecuadorian citizen who is a teacher of high school English and live on a 90 acre ranch solar powered and wind powered, off the grid and my four adopted children are home schooled by my Cheyenne wife and we live as Native American off the rez and pray to the creator for all our brothers and sisters and for the children in this time of home land madness and try to remember to honor our ancestor and all our relations, blessings, diego davalos."

Lucille Lang Day is the author of four poetry collections: *Infinities, Wild One, Fire In the Garden,* and *Self-Portrait With Hand Microscope,* which received the Joseph Henry Jackson Award in Literature. She also has a poetry chapbook in the "Greatest Hits" series from Pudding House Publications. She is director of the Hall of Health, a museum in Berkeley.

Diane di Prima is one of the few women Beat writers to come to prominence as a major literary force. Her memoir of the bohemian life in Greenwich Village in the 50s, *Memoirs of a Beatnik* is an American classic. Her books of poetry *Revolutionary Letters* and *Loba* are landmarks in our literary history. Her most recent book is *Recollections of My Life As A Woman: The New York Years.*

Paul Gandhi Joseph Dosh teaches political science at San Quentin prison and the University of California. His poems appear in *Soundings* (U.K.), the anthology *September 11: Contexts and Consequences* (Berkeley), and his chapbook *Provoke A New Hunger: An Activist's Handbook.* (*pablo@socrates.berkeley.edu*)

Tish Eastman is a songwriter, composer and writer. Her articles in the field of audio for media have appeared in various publications. Tish has won prizes for her poetry from Poetry in Windows IV and San Gabriel Valley Poets Quarterly and was a featured reader at the LA Poetry Festival.

Mariah Erlick is twelve years old and lives in the rural town of Willits, California. She enjoys reading and writing. Her interests are geared towards science, specifically genetics, although she also finds anthropology fascinating.

Lawrence Ferlinghetti was San Francisco's first Poet Laueate. His first book *Coney Island of The Mind* is probably the most widely read book of poetry in the world. He is the Founder of City Lights Books and the publisher of Allen Ginsberg's *Howl.* He continues to turn out wonderful books of poems and also has become a well known artist.

Jack Foley's books include the poetry collections *Exiles, Adrift,* and *Gershwin* and the companion critical volumes, *O Powerful Western Star* and *Foley's Books.* His radio show, *Cover to Cover,* is heard every Wednesday on Berkeley station, KPFA; his column, *Foley's Books,* appears weekly in the online magazine, *The Alsop Review.*

CB Follett's most recent poetry book, At the *Turning of the Light* won the 2001 National Poetry Book Award from Salmon Press, which published it. Nominated for 5 Pushcart Prizes, she is also the Editor/Publisher/General

Dogsbody of Arctos Press a publisher of poetry books, and is co-editor with Susan Terris of *Runes, A Review of Poetry*, a themed poetry annual. She is also an artist with work in many private and public collections both nationally and internationally.

Gail Ford woke up in 1988 to realize she had been writing for 25 years, and decided perhaps she could start writing consciously. Her goal for her first writing class was "to read a poem out loud and not die of embarrassment." Since then she has written, read in public, participated in and co-led workshops, hosted a poetry series, and become a small press publisher, and graduated (slowly, oh so slowly) to calling herself a writer. Visit her at and find out about activities for Bay Area writers, co-hosted by Gail, her husband poet/teacher Clive Matson, and their five-year-old son, Ezra.

Denis Fritzinger is Poetry Editor, *Earth First! Journal* and has been Published in *Earth First!*, *Wild Earth*, and *City Lights Anthology*. He is Co-founder, Warrior Poets Society.

Gary Mex Glazner is the author of, *Ears on Fire, Snapshot Essays in a World of Poets*, on La Alameda Press. It chronicles a year abroad in Asia and Europe with poems, translations and photos. In the spring of 2003 Sherman Asher Press will publish his book, *The Road Less Traveled: How to Make your Living as a Poet*.

S.A. Griffin is a Vietnam era vet, father, husband and eternal fool. Co-editor of *The Outlaw Bible of American Poetry*. Carma Bum. Crash vampire living in Los Angeles.

Tom Guarnera is 51 and lives and writes in the New York metropolitan area. He is a recent prizewinner in the Bay Area Poets Coalition annual poetry competition, and will be represented in 2003 in *Off the Cuffs*, an anthology of poems about the police. "Words, Like Survivors" appears in his collection, *For Better or Verse*, published by Rogue Scholars Press (New York).

Johnny Gunn is semi retired from a long career as reporter, editor, and publisher. "Among my favorite memories are the several years I spent as editor and publisher of *The Virginia City Legend*, a weekly newspaper published in Virginia City, Nevada, home to the fabulous Comstock Lode." His work has been published in *ByLine Magazine* (Flash Fiction Contest. Honorable Mention. July, 2002) *Tamafyhr Mountain Poetry* (Poem. Issue 12, May, 2002) among others.

Marj Hahne is a poet and an educator who teaches poetry writing to children and adults. She has performed her poetry in Philadelphia, New York, San Francisco, and Houston and Austin, Texas. Marj's poems have been published in *Painted Bride Quarterly, Mad Poets Review, La Petite Zine, Bum Rush the Page: A Def Poetry Jam* anthology, and *Off the Cuffs,* an anthology of poems by and about cops. She has recorded a poetry CD entitled *notspeak.*

Sam Hamill is Founding Editor at Copper Canyon Press. His books include *Gratitude* and *Dumb Luck* (recent poems) and *Destination Zero: Poems 1970-1995.* Among his dozens of volumes of poetry in translation are *Crossing the Yellow River: 300 Poems from the Chinese,* Lu Chi's third century *Art of Writing,* and *Narrow Road to the Interior & Other Writings* of Basho.

Sam Hamod was nominated for the Pulitzer Prize in Poetry in 1980; he has published 10 books of poems; he has also taught creative writing at The Writers Workshop of the U. of Iowa (Iowa City, IA), Princeton, Michigan, Wisconsin and Howard; he is the former editor and publisher of *Third World News* (Wash, DC); he has had talk shows on Pacifica radio in D.C. He is a frequent guest on talk shows in Wash DC, NYC and in the San Diego area discussing terrorism, the Middle East, world affairs and contemporary poetry.

QR Hand is a noted San Francisco jazz poet and often performs his work with jazz accompaniment. But even when he solos it sounds like jazz.

Karen Harlan "I am the oldest of sixteen children. I have three grown children and three grandchildren. I received my B. A. Degree in English from Southern llinois University, Carbondale, IL on May 10, 2002. I hope to return to do some graduate study."

Haleh Hatami was born to an American mother and an Iranian father. She received degrees in Middle Eastern Studies and in History from the University of California at Berkeley and the University of Chicago. She is currently enrolled in San Francisco State University's MFA Program in Creative Writing and lives in Oakland.

George Held is co-editor of *The Ledge.* His latest books are a collection of poems, *Beyond Renewal* (Cedar Hill, 2001), and the anthology *Touched By Eros* (2002), which he edited. He reviews poetry for *The Philadelphia Inquirer* and *The American Book Review,* among other periodicals.

Thea Hillman's writing has appeared in the *San Francisco Bay Guardian*, *Berkeley Review of Fiction*, *On Our Backs*, and the *Noirotica* series. She performed a birdcall on *The Tonight Show*, was on the cover of the *Oakland Phone Book*, but is most proud of her tag-team haiku championship title. My book, *Depending on the Light*, was published by Manic D Press in 2001.

Jack Hirschman lives in San Francisco and often travels and lives in Europe. His many books including *Lyripol* published by City Light. He is known as a poet of the people and is probably one of America's greatest though not widely known poets. He has translated more than thirty-five books of poetry from eight languages, including Italian, Albanian, Russian, Spanish, Greek, German, French, and Creole. He is in Europe reading (Summer and fall 2002). Fifty years of his poems, *Frontlines*, has just appeared, in the pocket poets series of City Lights.

J.Y. Ho is a student at San Diego State University, bday 2-27-81, home: Fullerton, California.

Karen Karpowich is a native New Yorker, who came to writing late in life. In recent years she has worked with some fine women poets and writers at "The Writer Voice" in New York. Some of her teachers and mentors have been Mary Stewart Hammond, Hermine Meinhard, Donna Masini and Wang Ping. Professionally she also spent her time working as an advertising executive and in recent years at iVillage.com, one of the leading destinations for women on the Internet. Her work has appeared online most recently on about.com's poetry newsletter. She is soon to be published in *Our Journey*.

Miki Kashtan grew up in Israel. In 1974, at the age of 18, she entered her two-year compulsory military service. Miki left Israel in 1983, unwilling to give her support to the continued war perpetuated in her name. In 1994 she joined the Veterans Writing Group with Maxine Hong Kingston, recognizing it as the first place where she could work through what she endured in her army years. Miki has dedicated her life to teaching nonviolence in word and spirit, hoping to contribute to a world where everyone's needs are met peacefully.

Jeff Kass is a teacher of English and Creative Writing at Pioneer High School in Ann Arbor, MI. He also directs the Creative Writing Program at Ann Arbor's Teen Center, The Neutral Zone, where he founded The Ann Arbor Youth Poetry Slam and *No Comment* magazine, and currently advises the nationally recognized *Volume Youth Poetry Project*. He was the Ann Arbor

Grand Slam Poetry Champion in 1999 and 2000 and the runner-up in 2001 and has performed his work to audiences all over the country. His partner Karen is a crew coach at The University of Michigan and their daughter Sam likes The Lorax.

Donna Suzanne Kerr was born in Boston, she now lives in Willits, California where she is the local librarian. Ms. Kerr's first poetry collection is *Between The Sword And The Heart: Tarot Poems.* Her second chapbook, a collection of haiku, is currently in publication. Ms. Kerr holds an MLS degree from the University of California, Berkeley.

Debra Khattab is the descendant of a three hundred year old American family that arrived a few years after the Mayflower. Her first husband was Palestinian and her current is Jewish. She has three children and is majoring in both Physics and English. She has published a chapbook, *Eavesdropping on Women Without Faces* and has hosted poetry readings in Berkeley and Oakland, California.

Traci Kato-Kiriyama is a performance artist/writer. She works with an LA-based trio, Zero 3, in their original touring show "Zero 3 – Stage and Spoken Word Superheroes." She is Producer and Curator of "Tuesday Nights at the Cafe", a bi-monthly multi-disciplinary artists venue in Little Tokyo, downtown Los Angeles.

Steve Kowit is an American Jewish poet who is passionately committed to the liberation of the Palestinian people. His only religious observance is to pray fervently for a regime change in Washington. An animal rights advocate, he has no doubt that dogs have Buddha-nature, but is far less certain about *Homo satanicus.*

Mark S. Kuhar is an Ohio-based writer & poet. His fiction & poetry have appeared in *Whiskey Island, Centerlight, The American Srbobran, Ohio Online, Big Bridge and Sidereality.* He has read his work on National Public Radio & does spoken word performance in his hometown of Cleveland. His nonfiction has appeared in a wide variety of local & national business, consumer & on-line publications. He is also the editor of *Deep Cleveland Junkmail Oracle,* a literary e-zine dedicated to the spirit of legendary Cleveland outlaw poet & underground publisher D.A Levy.

Meredith Karen Laskow is a New York native who has lived in Southern California since 1980. A prolific writer since her youth, she did not read publicly or send her work out for publication until two years ago. Response has generally been favorable. Ms. Laskow works as a jewelry artist and also teaches exercise classes for cancer survivors.

Teresa G. Lee is a bilingual poet -English/ Spanish who combines a dual career with teaching Spanish at the college level. She has been published in numerous anthologies, magazines and journals of poetry. Her recent book entitled *Twenty Love poems* is a bilingual effort to convey in two languages her thoughts on love in the 21st century .

Lyn Lifshin loves Abysinnian cats, writing poems, films, ballet— she has a new Aby, Jete Pentiment — her last, Memento died at 20 1/2. Her last two books were from Black Sparrow *Cold Comfort* and *Before It's Light.* The new one, *Another Woman Who Looks Like Me* from Black Sparrow/David Godine. She was near the Pentagon at a ballet class in the smoke of 9/11.

Leza Lowitz was born in San Francisco in 1962 and escaped to Tokyo in 1989. She has published two books of poems, *Yoga Poems: Lines to Unfold By* (Stone Bridge Press, 2000) which received the PEN Oakland Josephine Miles Award for Best Book of Poetry 2001, and was a finalist for the Indie Best Poetry Award; and *Old Ways To Fold New Paper* (Wandering Mind Books, 1997). She lived in Japan for five years, and has published six books of translations, including the popular anthologies of contemporary Japanese women's poetry, *Other Side River* and *A Long Rainy Season* (Stone Bridge Press, 1994/5. She has just completed two novels set in Japan, and a collection of short stories.

Radomir Luza Jr. is a poet and writer who has been published widely, including seven chapbooks, and has read his work all over the country. He was in bed when the planes hit, but he will never forget the faces and images he later saw in the city that he loves. Luza has been married to fellow poet and artist Monica for three years. He lives in Jersey City, NJ, outside of NYC.

Eugenia Macer-Story is an internationally-recognized poet/playwright and visual artist whose new play *Ars Chronicon Sylvestre* will be produced by Theater For The New City, NYC, 9/12 through 9/29, 2002. She also works as a professional clairvoyant and research consultant.

devorah major became the 3rd Poet Laureate in San Francisco in April of 2002. She won the PEN Oakland Josephine Miles Award for Literary Excellence for *street smarts* (poetry - Curbstone Press - 1997) and the Black

Caucus of the American Library Association First Novelist award for *An Open Weave* (Seal Press- 1996). She has a second novel published, *Brown Glass Windows* (Curbstone Press 2002) and a third book of poetry, *with more than tongue* (Creative Arts Books, Inc. 2002). Her poems, short stories, and essays are available in a number of magazines and anthologies. She has taught poetry and creative writing as community artist-in-residence and/or college adjunct professor for over 20 years.

Eileen Malone recently won Pen Women's Della Crowder Miller Poetry Prize for a poem celebrating creative process which she believes must be brought forth and sharply honed as the weapon against destruction and plunder that it can and should be.

Carlos Martinez, 52, was born and raised in New York City's Spanish Harlem. He's resided in Seattle since 1979. He is a graduate of Trinity College in Hartford, Connecticut and the Antioch University MFA in Creative Writing Program. He has been published in various magazines nationwide and has had one chapbook, *An Unendurable Love*, published. He is presently a Lecturer teaching creative writing (short prose and poetry) at Western Washington University.

Matthew Mason "Moving back to Omaha after getting a few English degrees in California, I've been trying to help form a more solid poetry community here. Even so, I've somehow found it difficult to pay my rent with just poetry, so I pay my bills by doing audio work on a videophotography crew and working in group homes for mentally ill adults. My poems have recently appeared in *Diagram*, *Wisconsin Review*, *Minnesota River Review*, *Bovine Free Wyoming*, and *Mid-American Review*.

Clive Matson writes from the itch in his body, which is old hat, says his how-to-write text *Let The Crazy Child Write!* (New World Library, 1998), to the delight of writing workshops. *Squish Boots*, his seventh book of poems, was placed in the coffin of his mentor, John Wieners. "Delightful and penetrating at the same time, these poems are a revelation," comments Susan Griffin. John hasn't been heard from.

Charlotte McCaffrey was born in Mobile, Alabama. She moved to California after two decades in the Midwest. Her work has appeared or is forthcoming in *The Comstock Review*, *Porcupine Magazine*, *Sojourner*, *Sulphur River Literary Review*, *Women's Studies Quarterly*, *Writers' Forum* and others. Currently, she teaches a special education class in the San Francisco Bay area.

Michael McClure is one of America's greatest poets. His two recent books are *Rain Mirror* (New Directions), and *Plum Stones* (O Books). His new CD with Ray Manzarek, *There's a Word,* is available from emptymirrorbooks.com.

Laurie McKenna is a cross disciplinary artist. She has been making short experimental films and writing prose and poetry for 20 years in Massachusetts. She currently resides in Bisbee, Arizona. She has a webiste that presents much of her work.

Michael McLaughlin is a three time $17,000 California Arts Council grant recipient. He has worked for eleven years as an Artist-in-Residence at Atascadero State Hospital, a maximum security forensic facility, and as a Contract Artist with the California Department of Corrections and California Youth Authority (w/ incarcerated adults & youth). Originally from San Francisco, McLaughlin lives on the central California coast with his 12 year old trumpet-playing son. Currently he is working on his second novel, *Gang of One.*

David Meltzer has written well over 50 books in little more than 25 years. An integral figure in the California small press scene of the 1960's and 1970's, Meltzer has published most of his books through small presses such as City Lights, Unicorn Press, and Robert Hawley's Oyez Press. He was born in Rochester, New York, but spent some of his youth as a rock musician in Boston and, in the late 1960's in California. In addition to writing numerous collections of poetry, Meltzer has edited a number of anthologies and the significant collection of interviews, the *San Francisco Poets* (1971). He now teaches at New College in San Francisco.

Todd Mills lives and works in the LA area. He is married and has two children. His poetry and short stories have appeared in *Yellow Silk, Voices* and *On The Bus.* He is director of the *Beat Museum.org* on the Web and produced the documentary film *Timothy Leary is Dead.*

John Minczeski's most recent book, "Circle Routes," was published by Akron University Press in 2001. Recent poems in *Agni, Quarterly West, Mid-American Review* and elsewhere. He works as a poet-in-the-schools in Minnesota and also teaches in various colleges and universities around the state.

Craig Moore: I took a walk down Haight Street in the summer of love; later I hung in City lights; and I saw and met some of the poets that I admired; I live with my wife now in the high desert.

Daniel Abdal-Hayy Moore was born in 1940 in Oakland, California. His first book of poems, *Dawn Visions*, was published by Lawrence Ferlinghetti of City Lights Books, San Francisco, in 1964. Creator of The Floating Lotus Magic Opera Company in Berkeley, California from 1967-1969, he became a Muslim/Sufi in 1970, performed the Hajj in 1972, and lived in Morocco, Spain, Algeria and Nigeria. In 1996 he published *The Ramadan Sonnets*, and in 2002 a new book of poems, *The Blind Beekeeper*. He lives in Philadelphia.

Cory-Ellen Nadel is a poet, novelist, occasional storyteller and frequent coffee-drinker living in Brooklyn, NY. A certified EMT, she worked for four days at Ground Zero. She is an MFA student at Sarah Lawrence College, where last year her first day of classes was scheduled to be September 11th.

Neil Nakadate teaches in the Department of English at Iowa State University. His publications have appeared in *Aethlon, Flyway, Mississippi Quarterly, Western Humanities Review, Genre, Tennessee Studies in Literature, Annals of Internal Medicine*, and elsewhere; he has edited two books on Robert Penn Warren and written a critical study of Jane Smiley's fiction (University of South Carolina Press, 1999).

Gerald Nicosia, known as Jack Kerouac's biographer (*Memory Babe*) and the chronicler of Vietnam vets (*Home To War*), has led a secret life as a post-beat poet and novelist for several decades. He has also been a not-so-secret activist for peace since the days of the Vietnam War, and has often worked in tandem with *Born On the Fourth Of July* wheelchair vet Ron Kovic.

Sharon Olinka's poetry has appeared in *Long Shot, Onthebus, Poetry Wales*, and *Bum Rush the Page: A Def Poetry Jam*. She has performed her work at The Writer's Voice, Dixon Place, Beyond Baroque, and A Gathering of the Tribes, among other venues. She's the author of *A Face Not My Own*, from West End Press, and writes for American Book Review and thylazine.com.

Charles Pappas, 55, was born in Boston, Massachusettes and has lived in Berkeley since 1975. Upon becoming disabled in 1973 he left Philadelphia, where he worked as a community activist after attending the University of Pennsylvania, for the climate and benefits of the San Francisco Bay area. He has published 10 books of poetry (Regent Press), citing the spoken word poetry scene of the early 1990s as a wellspring of inspiration, especially praising his many fellow poets, artists and musicians of northern California for their talent, dedication and insights.

Robert Pinsky was United States Poet Laureate 1997-2000. He is continuing his work on the Favorite Poem Project, creating an audio and video archive featuring Americans from all walks of life reading aloud a beloved poem. He is the author of six books of poetry, most recently *Jersey Rain*, five books of criticism, and numerous translations. Pinsky is the poetry editor of *Slate* magazine and a regular contributor to "The News Hour with Jim Lehrer" on PBS. He teaches in the graduate writing program at Boston University.

Kenneth Pobo most recent chapbook *Kenneth Pobo's Greatest Hits* was published in June 2002 by Pudding House Press. Last year, Higganum Hills Books published his book called *Ordering: A Season in My Garden*. His work appears in: *Colorado Review, Mudfish, forpoetry.com, Indiana Review, Spectacle*, and elsewhere. His interests include gardening, collecting rare records from the 1960s, and films. He teaches creative writing and English at Widener University in Chester, Pennsylvania.

Janine Pommy Vega has worked for twenty years in arts in education programs in New York State, teaching grades K through 12 in English and Spanish with Alternative Literary Programs, Teachers & Writers, The Writer's Voice, The New York City Ballet, and Poets in The Schools; and teaching inmates in correctional facilities through Incisions/Arts. She is the author of twelve books and chapbooks since 1968. Her work has appeared in *The Village Voice, Baltimore Sun*, and *Mademoiselle* magazine. Her book, *Tracking The Serpent: Journeys to Four Continents*, a collection of essays on the Amazon, the Andes and Himalayas, was published by City Light Books

Jeff Poniewaz ia an eco-activist Jeff Poniewaz and teaches "Literature of Ecological Vision" via UW-Milwaukee. His *Dolphin Leaping in the Milky Way* (Inland Ocean, 1986) won him a PEN "Discovery Award." His "Sept. 11" poem forms the finale of his nextbook MS, which is seeking a publisher.

David Ray is author of several award-winning books. His latest, forthcoming from Holy Cow! Press, is *One Thousand Years—Poems About The Holocaust*. He lives with wife Judy and dogess Levi in Tucson, Arizona and travels widely giving readings and workshops.

Timothy Michael Rhodes is a Nevada poet and and member of Ash Canyon Poets. He has been published in *Red Wheelbarrow* and *River King*. His two main passions are music and poetry.

Dr. Skip Robinson consults and teaches psychology and conflict resolution at Sonoma State University and in other countries with the Conflict Resolution, Research, and Resource Institute (CRI). He served as President of the Board of California Poets in the Schools. His most recent books of poetry are *Standing on a Whale Fishing for Minnows* and *When Einstein, Dreaming, Rides the Beam of Light.*

Eugene Ruggles lives in Petaluma, CA . He says he has been 86d out of most bars on the West Coast while being nominated for the Pulitzer in poetry for *Lifeguard in the Snow* in 1978. He has received a National Endowment for the Arts Award, a Poetry Society of America award and others. His poetry has been published in the *New Yorker, Poetry Chicago,* and *Kayak.*

Ann Marie Sampson: "I guess I was born to write since I've been doing it almost all my life. When 9/11 happened, I was stunned silent and then wrote in my journal for days to cleanse my heart. This poem is part of what I wrote. I have had poems and stories published in various literary magazines. *ZZYZZYVA, Inkwell, Quixote Quarterly,* for examples. I live with my husband and extended family in Willits where I teach memoir writing to some pretty extraordinary human beings."

Mike Schneider lives in Pittsburgh and works as a science writer at Carnegie Mellon University. In off hours he is arts editor of *The New People,* a monthly activist newspaper published by the Thomas Merton Center of Pittsburgh. He has won awards for my free-lance journalism. His poems have appeared in many journals, recently including *5 AM, Atlanta Review, Notre Dame Review* and *Sycamore Review.* Work is forthcoming in *Poetry.*

Iris N. Schwartz, who studied writing at NYU and New School University, is a fiction writer and poet whose work has appeared in *Allspice, Blue Collar Review, Ducts, Ludlow Press, The Pikeville Review* and other print and on-line publications. She has performed on radio and on-line, interactive TV, as well as at many New York venues, including Barnes & Noble Booksellers, The College of Staten Island, KGB Bar, The Knitting Factory, and Remote Lounge. Ms. Schwartz promises, under threat of bodily harm by her protagonist, to finish her novel-in-progress, *Sirena Wailing,* as soon as she possibly can.

F. John Sharp lives in Aurora, Ohio and his work can be found in various publications, both in print and online, in the U.S and Europe. Contact him at fjsjr45@yahoo.com.

Carl Stilwell: "I'm a retired teacher who still continues to teach 1-2 days a week for for the Los Angeles Unified School District. The rest of the week I like to participate in local open poetry readings where I'm known as CaLokie. I have poems published in *Struggle, Verve, Pearl, Pemmican* and *Blue Collar Review*."

John Sinclair: Poet, performer, music journalist, award-winning radio programmer, record producer, former Professor of Blues History at Wayne State University in Detroit ... ex-Chairman of the White Panther Party, ex-manager of the MC-5, ex-political prisoner. Author of *Guitar Army; Music & Politics; This Is Our Music; Fire Music: A Record; Meditations: A Suite for John Coltrane,* and *We Just Change The Beat* ... the legendary John Sinclair continues to kick out the jams from his headquarters in New Orleans. You can find him touring the country with his jazz band The Blues Scholars or on WWOZ- FM in New Orleans. His elongated blues work in verse, *Fattening Frogs For Snakes,* is just out from Surregional Press, along with the CD of *Volume One: The Delta Sound* by John Sinclair & His Blues Scholars from Okra-Tone Records.

Elizabeth Turner is a Financial Adviser at UBS PaineWebber. This is her first published poem.

Ryan G. Van Cleave has taught creative writing and literature at the Florida State University, the University of Wisconsin-Madison, and the University of Wisconsin-Green Bay; he currently works as a freelance writer and editor in Green Bay, Wisconsin. His work is forthcoming in *The Harvard Review, The Iowa Review,* and *Ontario Review.* His most recent books include a poetry collection, *Say Hello* (Pecan Grove Press, 2001), an anthology, *Like Thunder: Poets Respond to Violence in America* (University of Iowa Press, 2002), and a creative writing textbook, *Contemporary American Poetry: Behind the Scenes* (Allyn & Bacon/Longman, 2003).

Julia Vinograd has published 47 books of poetry based on her experience and observation of life in the streets and cafes of Berkeley CA. She has an MA in Fine Arts from the University of Iowa. She has recorded three CDs of her poetry: Eye of The Hand; Bubbles and Bones and most recently Book of Jerusalem.

Scott Wannberg is a 49 year old independent bookstore employee who once rode shotgun with the Carma Bums poetry troupe, and is still amazed how his material dances forth from within.

Paula Nemeroff Weiss: Though she started writing poetry after her children were grown, a love of words and the need for self-expression began in early childhood. For the past five years Paula has been co-leader of a poetry workshop in Brea, California. She resides in Fullerton, California with her husband.

Pat Phillips West is a former hospital administrator/business owner who lives and writes in northern Nevada. Her work has appeared in an anthology, *Labyrinth: Poems and Prose*, as well as *FZQ Poetry, Poetictricity* (Kota Press), and *All Things Girl*.

Gerald R. Wheeler (Katy, Texas), is a Pushcart Prize nominee. His fiction, poetry, and photography have appeared in *North American Review, Kaleidoscope, Louisiana LIiterature, Pivot, Whole Terrain, Big Muddy, Vincent Brothers Review Connecticut River Review, Aethlon,* and elsewhere. His is the author of *Tracers* (Black Bear Publications) and soon to be published *Tracks* by Timberline Press.

A.D. Winans was born, raised and lives in San Francisco. Former Editor/Publisher of *Second Coming Magazine*/Press. Author of 30 books of poetry. Most recent book, just released by Dustbooks, *The Holy Grail: Charles Bukowski and the Second Coming Revolution.* Forthcoming book: *A Bastard Child With No Place To Go* (12 Gauge Press).

Dr. Bronwyn Winter is a Professor in the Department of French Studies at the University of Sydney, Australia. Her work on feminist theory, women in international and national politics, human rights, women and the politics of race, nation and culture, Islamism, globalization, lesbian politics, and critiques of liberalism has been widely published in Australian and international journals and anthologies. She also writes poetry, when the heavy demands of academia permit, and is active in the National Tertiary Education Union. She is, with Susan Hawthorne, co-editor of the book *September 11, 2001: Feminist Perspectives* (Melbourne, Spinifex 2002), in which her poem *Dislocations* was first published. She attended a women's conference associated with the Loya Jirga in Kabul, and visited UN and refugee camp and NGOs in Peshawar, and feminist and trade union organisations in Lahore.

Nellie Wong is a long-time socialist feminist activist and poet. She was born in the Year of the Dog in Oakland's Chinatown. The Bay Area Organizer for the Freedom Socialist Party, she's also active in Radical Women and the Town Hall Committee Against War and Hate. She's a lover of jazz, good food, and international films.

Al Young was born May 31, 1939 at Ocean Springs, Mississippi on the Gulf Coast near Biloxi. He grew up in the South and in Detroit. He travels internationally and extensively, reading, lecturing and often performing with musicians. His poetry and prose have been translated into Italian, Spanish, Swedish, Norwegian, Serbo-Croatian, Polish, Chinese, Japanese, Russian, German, and other languages. Current projects: *A Piece of Cake* (a novel), *Mad, Bad and Dangerous to Know: Or, Opus de Funk* (an account in verse of Lord Byron and Lady Caroline Lamb's infamous romance), a screen adaptation of *Seduction By Light*, his 1988 Hollywood novel); and volume two of *The Literature of California*, co-edited with scholar-critic Jack Hicks, and novelists James D. Houston and Maxine Hong Kingston.

Acknowledgements

Antler's *Skyscraper Apocalypse* excerpts were published in *The Sun*, Chapel Hill, N.C and September 11, 2001, *American Writers Respond*, Etruscan Press, edited by William Heyen.

Eva Yaa Asantewaa's *The Sacrament* was published in *The Pedestal Magazine* at http://www.thepedestalmagazine.com.

Claire Burch's *On the Fall of the World Trade Towers* was published in *Peace News*, September, 2001, San Francisco, edited by John Bryan and Allen Cohen.

Allen Cohen's *The Fallen Tower* was published in *Peace News*, September, 2001, San Francisco, edited by John Bryan and Allen Cohen.

Lucy Day's *Strangers* was published in *September 11, 2001: American Writers Respond* (Etruscan Press, 2002). Edited by William Heyen.

Paul Dosh's *No Such Thing As A Precision Bomb* was published *Soundings*, a U.K. journal and the UC Berkeley anthology *September 11: Contexts and Consequences.*

Tom Guarnera's *Words, Like Survivors* was published in his collection, *For Better or Verse*, published by Rogue Scholars Press, New York.

Sam Hamill's *The New York Poem* was published in *Dumb Luck*, BOA Editions, 2002.

Steve Kowit's *The Equation* was published in *September 11, 2001, American Writers Respond*, Etruscan Press, edited by William Heyen.

Eugenia Macer-Story's *WTC Boom Box: The Subway Joke Unsounded* was published in a chapbook *Carrying Thunder: Poems of Wonder* by Eugenia Macer-Story.

Michael McClure's *Black Dahlia* was published in *Peace News*, San Francisco, CA September 2001 and in *Enough*, O Books, Oakland, CA.

Daniel Abdal-Hayy Moore's *The Little Ramshackle Shack* was published in the magazine *Long Shot*, Volume 25, 2002.

Neil Nakadate's *Time and Place* was published in the Fall 2002 issue of *Cottonwood*.

Gerry Nicosia's *The Bell Tolls Again* was published in *Peace News*, September 2001.

Sharon Olinka's *It Must Not Happen* appeared on *Big City Lit* website.

Robert Pinsky's *Newspaper* was published in *American Poetry Review*.

Jeff Poniewaz's *September 11, 2000* excerpts published in *September 11, 2001, American Writers Respond*, Etruscan Press, edited by William Heyen.

John Sinclair's *Ask Me Now* was published in *thelonious: a book of monk*, © 2002 John Sinclair.

Carl Stilwell's *We the People* was published in the San Gabriel Valley Poetry Journal, Winter 2001.

Judith Terzi's *Gate 6A* was published in *Shiny Things Make Things Come Back*, Small Poetry Press in May, 2002.

Juanita Torrence-Thompson's *Naseem* was published in *The Pedestal Magazine.com*.

Gerald Wheeler's *The Weavers* was published in *Black Bear Review*.

Gerald Wheeler's *Burka Women* will be published in *Apostrophe*.

A.D Winan's *Front Row Seat in Heaven* appeared in *Beat Blue Jacket*, Japan.

Dr. Bronwyn Winter's *Kabul* is part of a longer work, *Dislocations published in September 11, 2001: Feminist Perspectives* ed. Susan Hawthorne and Bronwyn Winter. Melbourne: Spinifex.

Al Young's *Held Captive* was published in *Peace News, September, 2001*, San Francisco, edited by John Bryan and Allen Cohen.